MEMORIES OF A NORTHERN CHILDHOOD

Josephine Cox was born in Blackburn, one of ten children. At the age of sixteen, Josephine met and married her husband Ken, and had two sons. When the boys started school, she decided to go to college and eventually gained a place at Cambridge University. She was unable to take this up as it would have meant living away from home, but she went into teaching – and started to write her first full-length novel. She won the 'Superwoman of Great Britain' Award, for which her family had secretly entered her, at the same time as her novel was accepted for publication.

Josephine says, 'I love writing, both recreating scenes and characters from my past, together with new storylines which mingle naturally with the old. I could never imagine a single day without writing, and it's been that way since as far back as I can remember.'

Piers Dudgeon is the author of fifteen works of non-fiction. He worked for ten years as a publisher before starting his own company and developing books with authors as diverse as John Fowles, Ted Hughes, Daphne du Maurier, Catherine Cookson and Peter Ackroyd. In 1993 he moved to a village on the North Yorkshire Moors where he has written a number of books, including biographies of Sir John Tavener, Edward de Bono and Catherine Cookson, *The Girl from Leam Lane* becoming a no. 1 bestseller.

Visit ... nation on yo ...

By the same author:

Catherine Cookson Country

Dickens' London

The English Vicarage Garden

Dear Boy: Lord Chesterfield's Letters to his Son

Village Voices: A Portrait of Change 1915–1990

Daphne du Maurier: Enchanted Cornwall

The Country Child: An Illustrated Reminiscence

The Spirit of Britain: An Illustrated Guide to Literary Britain

The Girl from Leam Lane: The Life and Works of Catherine Cookson

Josephine Cox: Memories of a Northern Childhood

Breaking Out Of The Box: The Biography of Edward de Bono

Lifting the Veil: The Biography of Sir John Tavener

Kate's Daughter: The Real Catherine Cookson

The Woman of Substance: The Life and Works of Barbara Taylor Bradford

Child of the North

MEMORIES OF A
NORTHERN CHILDHOOD

Piers Dudgeon with
Josephine Cox

HarperCollins*Publishers*

HarperCollins*Publishers*
77–85 Fulham Palace Road,
Hammersmith, London W6 8JB

www.**harpercollins**.co.uk

This revised and updated edition 2006
11

First published in Great Britain by
Headline 2001

A catalogue record for this book
is available from the British Library

ISBN 0 00 720278 4

Typeset in Linotype Sabon by
Rowland Phototypesetting Ltd, Bury St Edmunds, Suffolk

Printed and bound in Great Britain by
Clays Ltd, St Ives plc

CONTENTS

FOREWORD
by Josephine Cox

I thought I knew all there was to know about the land of my birth. I now realise that I was wrong.

This wonderful, in-depth book, meticulously re-searched and written by Piers Dudgeon, has opened my eyes to a world I never really knew, with many places and events that were inevitably beyond my experience. My own private, precious little world was the backstreets of Blackburn town, and the magical Corporation Park, where I played out many childish dramas in my imagination.

Deprived and confined though my world was, it was never quiet or uneventful, and for all its inherent difficulties I would not want to change it. I could never deny my upbringing, because it is who I am; my roots are firmly embedded in those difficult, frus-trating, wonderful days, when food was short and 'nice' clothes were what someone else wore.

It has been said that your childhood moulds and makes you the person you are, and I believe this is true. It's why today, and for the rest of my life, I will never take things for granted. Each and every value and principle I nurture has sprung directly from my background. Added to that, it gave me the stories I write: stories of human beings, and emotions, and the knowledge that when life knocks you down, the only way back is to stand tall and straight and look it in the eye.

The whole of my childhood is like a moving picture in my mind. I loved every inch of the narrow cobbled streets. With their many pubs and churches, pawn shops and little houses, they throbbed with life. The square-headed, black-coated lamps quietly guarded the pavements by day and lit the way home for lovers and drunks of a night-time. The back-to-back houses with their tiny *Coronation Street* yards and outside cold, damp lavvies (situated in a discreet corner beside the midden hole) held many a naughty or dangerous secret behind the twitching net curtains. Secrets I carried into my adult life and which I now retell in my stories.

The people were warm and friendly, and every mother was mother to every child in the street, regardless of which house a child might live in. The men worked hard and the women bore the children, and life was hectic and noisy, and often violent.

Our own house bustled with children, but, thinking back, I was never really a child. That would have been far too easy. But children should be innocent, and as my Grandma Harrison would say, 'be seen and not heard.' That was not me. I watched and listened and learned.

My Blackburn was a wonderful place, with smoking chimneys that darkened the skies and mill whistles piercing the air, calling the folk to work. These 'folk' were 'real' flesh-and-blood people. A great number of the same kind of people remain to this day, though many of the familiar landmarks I knew have long since gone. There was a loud, colourful market where the men shouted their wares, and the women from the seaside would sell their shrimps and other shellfish from the depths of a wicker basket. The market was large and sprawling, with a splendid, sturdy clock that stood tall and proud in the centre and could be seen from one corner of the marketplace to the other. On a weekend evening, its large, smiling face looked down on the meeting of friends and sweethearts. No doubt it could have told many a tale, which we will never know because, sadly, some years later, the planners in their infinite 'wisdom' saw fit to demolish this wonderful landmark.

There were other memorable 'landmarks' in my young life. The Ragged School, 'Founded in the Cause of Christian Love and Fellowship' and 'Opened by Mayor John Truman, July 15th, 1942', where Christian people offered practical help and comfort to the children from poorer backgrounds than their own. There was the Cicely Bridge Mill, where I would go to meet our mam after school; and Nazareth House, where she would take us when things were not going so well financially. The nuns there were kind and generous, something I have never forgotten. There was the slaughter-house, near where, for some time, we lived – and the awful smell permeated the air day and night. This is one particular memory I would prefer to erase, but which, like the others, is stored in my soul for all time.

One other unforgettable incident happened on a chilly morning in February 1952. I was playing in the street, when suddenly everybody rushed out of their houses, some in tears and others eager to spread the shocking news that King George had died. The street went into mourning, as did the whole country, but to me and every other child it was something that affected only the adults. We looked and wondered, and cried when our parents cried, but being children we did not seem directly touched by this sad, historic event. And yet it is a day I will never forget, because of the emotion that swept through my little world and, for a time, carried me along.

Many years later, circumstances beyond my control carried me away from my beloved Blackburn, and in so doing brought me together with Ken, my sweetheart and subsequently my husband and friend.

It is well-known that my family means a great deal to me. In spite of my mam and dad going their different ways, I remain ever close to my sisters and the brothers it broke my heart to leave behind. I love them all now as I did then: without reservation.

I give my heartfelt thanks to Piers Dudgeon for his hard work and memorable account of the North of England in this book. I know he spent many hours driving about and walking the streets of Blackburn, researching wherever he could and chatting to anyone who had things to tell him. At the end of it, he has written a very special account of the way it was and some incidents of childhood. And though this is not my life story, it shows a glimpse of my early days, and I am proud to be part of it all.

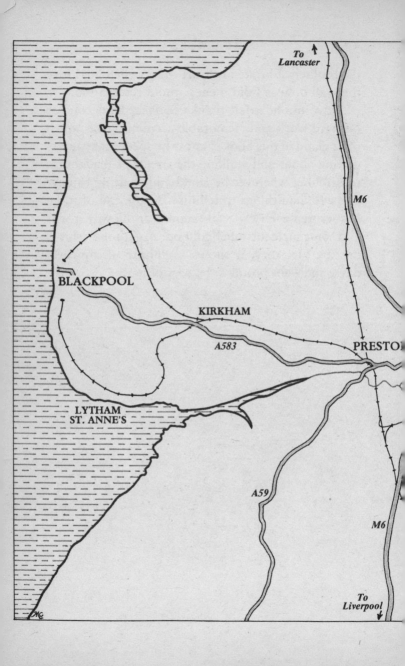

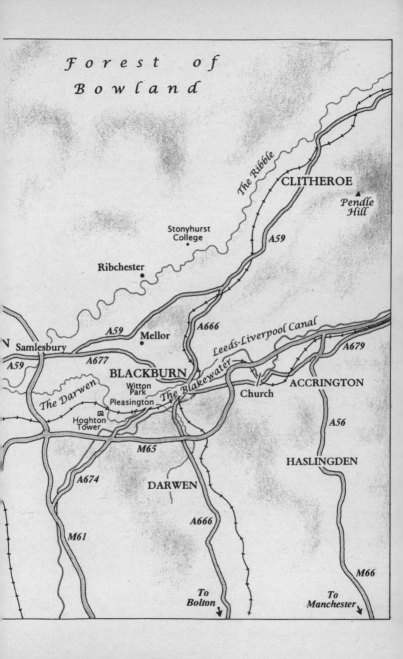

INTRODUCTION

Images from Blackburn in the 1940s and '50s propel us into a microcosmic world of Josephine Cox's childhood: a red Oxo tin; a mangle roller; a long, narrow glass of sarsaparilla; an old wireless resting on a lace doily in the corner of the front room; the ubiquitous gas-lamp. People relate to Jo's fictional world because it is ground out of a reality that she knew only too well in the first fourteen years of her life, and she clings to symbolic elements of it, such as sarsaparilla, a forerunner to Coca Cola, which is drunk by her characters relentlessly whether they are living in the 1950s or much later.

Jo was born in 1941, in an old cotton-mill house on a cobbled street long gone to progress. 'It was a slum and life was a struggle,' she has said. There were seven boys and three girls in the family; two more children were lost in infancy. Jo was number four.

Her childhood was characterful, seamless, and independent of the wider world. This is reflected in her novels, as Queenie's amazement shows when

Biddy suggests a trip to nearby Blackpool in *Her Father's Sins*: 'Outside Blackburn, Auntie Biddy? Are we going outside Blackburn?' For the town's occupants, until Nosey-Parker Hindle purchased the first TV in Blackburn in 1952, the world beyond Blackburn didn't exist.

Her Father's Sins, Jo's first novel, is a masterly, child's-eye view of her upbringing in the 1940s and '50s, but her work is not simply an extension of her own childhood past for reminiscence's sake. She is working things out, mythologising, and also sorting through her own feelings about what has passed. *Angels Cry Sometimes*, her fourth novel, is based on her mother's struggle. Her father, Barney Brindle, was employed by Blackburn Council on the roads, and, like others frustrated by life at the tail-end of the Industrial Revolution, he drank away his wages in the pub on a Friday night and sometimes vented his frustration in rages that terrified his children. At home, Jo's mother, Mary Jane Harrison, survivor of the cotton mills, somehow kept the family together until Jo was fourteen, when she walked out, taking some of her children with her. These events, and in particular Jo's loss of her father at such a crucial moment in her development, are as important to her fiction as the environment in which her childhood took place and of which, as we will see, they are an integral part. Her novels also take us farther back in time, so that we can see how that environment came into being. These were exciting, innovative times, as Jo observed in her novel, *Outcast*:

> Cotton mills were going up at an unprecedented rate all over Lancashire, but here in Blackburn the programme of mill construction was staggering. Emma had inherited her papa's own pride in these great towering monstrosities, and she knew all their names – Bank Top Mill, Victoria Mill, Infirmary Mill – and, oh, so many more! Cotton was big business, keeping the town a hive of bustling activity. No hardworking mill-hand ever grew rich by it as his wages were too meagre; but, for the man with money to invest, the opportunities grew day by day . . .

The series of inventions that triggered the Industrial Revolution speeded up first the spinning, then the weaving processes. They included the flying shuttle, the spinning jenny, the water frame, the spinning mule, the steam engine and the power loom. Then new transport systems – the railway and the canal – to and from ports at Liverpool, London and eventually Manchester vastly improved the supply and distribution network.

The earliest mills in Blackburn, such as Wensley Fold Mill (1775), King Street Mill (1817) and

Whalley Banks Mill (1818), were opened to house the new spinning machines.

These mills represented a whole different way of life. Workers no longer owned their own wheels; instead of working in their own homes at their own pace, spinners would now have to work in their employers' factories at the machines' pace for new entrepreneurial masters. Many were drawn in from outlying villages, as livelihoods were threatened by the factory operations.

By 1800 there were seven thousand such operatives in Blackburn, representing around sixty per cent of the population. Twenty years later the number had more than doubled – a body of workers nearly 15,000 strong represented almost seventy per cent of the town's burgeoning population.

The coming of the power loom greatly accelerated this shift from country to town. Power looms were first installed in Blackburn at Dandy Mill in 1825, from which time the writing was on the wall for hand-loomers. In the town's most authoritative history, *Blackburn: The Development of a Lancashire Cotton Town,* Derek Beattie charts the transition as follows. In 1780, Blackburn's population was five thousand. In 1801, it amounted to 11,980, with seven thousand hand looms in use. In 1841 there were some six thousand power looms in use and possibly as few as one thousand hand looms. In 1907, Blackburn was the cotton-weaving capital of the world; there were around 130,000 people, no hand looms, but 79,403 power looms in use.

Aiding and abetting production improvements was the new transport system. In 1770, building work began on the Leeds–Liverpool canal.

The Leeds to Liverpool Canal was a main artery from the Liverpool Docks to the various mills. Along this route the fuel and raw cotton which kept the mills alive was brought, thus affording a living to the many bargees who, with their families, dwelt in their colourful floating homes and spent most of their lives travelling to and from with their cargoes. This consisted mainly of raw cotton, unloaded from ships which carried it across the ocean from America.

Jo's novel, *Outcast*, quoted above, tells us much about the workings of industry in the nineteenth century. The canal, which would run commercial traffic until 1972, reached Blackburn in 1810, easing transportation not only of raw cotton and cloth, but of coal, lime and building materials mined in the neighbourhood – goods for powering the cotton industry and enabling the building programme that would be so closely bound up with it. In the more recent *Bad Boy Jack* we get a time-honoured picture of a barge 'moved along, pulled by a massive horse, loaded down with cargo and painted colourfully from stem to stern.' But it is Emma Grady in *Outcast*, who takes us inside one of these great boats:

It was the first time Emma had ever been inside a barge, and it had been a great surprise. Not for a moment had she expected to see such a cosy and exceptionally pretty home as this. All the walls and ceiling were made of highly polished panels. In the living-quarters the walls were decorated with lovely brass artefacts – plates, old bellows and the like; from the ceiling hung three oil-lamps of brass and wood, each sparkling and meticulously kept; there were two tiny dressers, both made of walnut and displaying small china ornaments – which, according to Sal, were 'put away when we're on the move'; as were the china plates which were propped up on shelves beneath each porthole; the horse-hair chairs were free-standing, but the dressers were securely fixed to the floorboards. There was also a small cast-iron fire, and the narrow galley which was well-stocked and spotless. In one of the two bedrooms there was a tiny dresser with a tall cupboard beside it, and a deep narrow bunk beneath a porthole. Emma had been astonished

6

that everything a person might need could be provided in such a limited space.

The railway was the next fillip to industry, the Preston–Blackburn line opening in 1846. However, it was never the dominant force that the canal turned out to be, as Mike Clarke notes in Alan Duckworth's *Aspects of Blackburn*. In 1851 the canal's cargo business was leased to a group of local railway companies, including the Lancashire and Yorkshire Railway, which gave it a virtual monopoly on transport in East Lancashire. Mill owners, increasingly ill-served by this monopoly, pressured the canal company to revoke the lease. By 1880 the Lancashire and Yorkshire Railway was laying off staff at Burnley because the canal had taken over much of their traffic. As a result, new boatyards sprang up and business boomed in those that were already servicing the canal.

In *Vagabonds*, Marlow Tanner builds up a canal cargo business – Tanner's Transporters – and is part of this new boatyard boom:

He had worked his way up from being a bargee who struggled for a living, going cap-in-hand to such men as Caleb Crowther who once owned most of the mills along the wharf – property that, by rights, had belonged to Emma . . . You'll never find a better gaffer than Marlow Tanner.

The new inventions in the cotton industry increased the speed of production and made it more economical. The improved transport enhanced supply of raw cotton and distribution of finished cloth. In 1913, Lancashire as a whole could boast exports of seven billion yards of cloth.

The first mill-worker housing in Blackburn sprang up around Wensley Fold, Blackburn's first spinning mill, close to where Josephine Cox was born. Seven cottages appeared in 1809, numbers rapidly increasing so that by 1832 the mill master had built eighty-four houses around and about. The mill owned your house, many of the shops in the area and the pub at the end of the road. The master paid your wages and then mopped them up again in any way he could.

Three main mill colonies shaped the burgeoning town from the 1820s: Brookhouse to the northeast, Nova Scotia to the south, and Grimshaw Park to the southeast. By 1847 these colonies had grown so large that they accounted for a third of employment in the cotton industry. These worker colonies comprised endless, closed-in rows of terraced housing, two rooms upstairs, two rooms down, no bathroom, no hot water except that which was boiled in the kettle, no front garden, a backyard scarcely big enough to turn round in and an outside lavatory backing onto a narrow passage. Some of the earliest terraces were back-to-backs with no alleyway between, but it soon became apparent that these posed appalling sanitation and health risks.

Over the following decades, the character of the Blackburn spinners and weavers was challenged by harsh discipline, by regular depressions in the industry, by general poverty and the often appalling conditions in which they had to live and work. The town would become a centre of manufacture for the world, but it would also become a cesspit of human misery, before it began its painful and terminal wind-down, which saw up to fifty per cent of the workforce unemployed in 1930, and by 1957 a two-thirds reduction of its cotton mills, right down to one working mill – Witton Mill in Stancliffe Street – all that is left today.

In *Her Father's Sins*, class or poverty levels are measured by the number of gas-lamps in a street, each inscribed with a carving of the Lancaster Rose. We will see that class differentiation and interplay in Blackburn was subtly and strategically staged, so that the mill masters were able to count on the support of the workers, on whose labours they became rich, by engineering a code of loyalty or team spirit akin to that of a modern-day football fan to football club, as if the masters shared the same purpose and values as their workers – which, of course, they did, didn't they? Only a perceptive few saw the nature of the fraud at the time.

In the mid-twentieth century when Jo Cox was

growing up in Blackburn, a quarter of the working population were still engaged in textiles, especially weaving. But it was a much reduced industry, the routine of life giving the appearance of continuity, the daily shape that linked 1950s Blackburn to an age-old tradition of cotton and ale – from the five a.m. rat-a-tat of the knocker-up's stick to the end of a back-breaking day, laughing and singing in the pubs, which held pride of place in every lamp-lined cobbled street.

There had in fact been change in every generation since the Industrial Revolution took hold. The cold, relentless march of progress occurred in every era, and in the 1950s, change was once again round the corner. With it would come the slum-clearance and rebuilding programme in which Mr Marsden has a hand in *Her Father's Sins*, and new inhabitants too: 'If somebody 'ad offered me the bloody Crown Jewels some five years back, against a body swappin' the land o' sunshine to come to Blackburn, I'd never have taken the bet!' Today the ethnic Asian population accounts for more than a fifth of the town's inhabitants.

In the meantime, for many more indigenous families in the 1940s and early 1950s (Jo's included), poverty was the harsh reality, and the coming of the Welfare State brought no miracle cure. 'Poverty, real degrading poverty, had crept up on them,' Jo writes in *Her Fathers Sin's*, and was symbolised by the Cob o' Coal: 'Nine feet tall with a skirt dimension of twenty feet or more, it was raw and shiny black, hard as the day it was wrestled out by the miners from its long resting place beneath the ground.' Raw rock-coal, unsuitable for burning, it had been given a shiny brass plaque and transported to its place at the corner of Pump Street and Waterfall Mill to the accompaniment of the town band. However, the need of the poor folk was such that within six years it had been reduced to a hump-backed deformity of which no one could be proud.

With money short and up to twelve at table, life at home for Jo's family was hard, and the indignities hurtful (she was teased at school for her pawnshop clothes). Hand in hand with poverty ('when optimism was a luxury') came drunkenness. Jo has declared that the fictional George Kenny's appalling drunken rages (*Her Father's Sins*) are based on her experience of her own father. Her parents brought out the worst in each other, and Kelly's feelings in *Somewhere, Someday* about her father ruining her mother's life were Jo's.

Poverty is also linked to ill-health – Biddy dies of consumption in *Her Father's Sins*. It brings us, too, to the role of religion in the community: to Father Riley, to the Blackburn Ragged School, to the Salvation Army and to the Convent of Nazareth House, which played such a part in Jo's life even after 'the Welfare' had taken hold in the town. The levels of poverty point, too, to other elements in the cultural stew: to manipulation, exploitation, abuse, rape, illegitimacy and incest. All are recurring themes in Jo's novels. Incest was a particular problem in such very crowded living conditions even in the last century.

Love within the family is a preoccupation of the novels. In *Jinnie*, the mother figure, Louise Hunter, adopts a child who is the product of a one-time union between her late husband Ben and her own sister, Susan. In *Cradle of Thorns*, Lilian has an unrequited incestuous desire for her brother, Don Reece. In *Jessica's Girl*, Noreen suspects Edward of making his sister Jessica pregnant. In *Her Father's Sins*, the word is that Sheila Thorogood's baby is her twin brother Raymond's, and Queenie (in many ways a dead ringer for Jo) falls in love with Richard Marsden, not knowing that they share the same father in George Kenney: 'I love Rick with all my heart. I want no other; and so it seems I'm determined to be forever lonely. I can't pretend to understand your ways, God, but I hope You can understand me; and find it in Your heart to forgive me my sin tonight.'

In *Let Loose the Tigers*, Sheila, with her heart of gold, advises Queenie to go to Rick, brother or not – 'yer love each other, wrong or right . . .' While in *Born to Serve* it is the father's incest with the daughter that is examined. Claudia threatens her mother that she will tell the world, 'Your husband bedded me . . . his own daughter. I'm carrying his child!' In *Her Father's Sins*, drink is the expediter of similar shocking invasion on the part of George Kenney:

> *Gasping for breath, Queenie fought with every ounce of strength she could summon. But the powerful brutality of her attacker rendered her helpless and the horror which smothered her screaming became unbearable.*
>
> *Tearing aside her flimsy nightwear and shattering the golden-heart chain about her delicate throat, George Kenney in his brutality took his own child's virgin innocence, with no thought of consequence or compassion, his own lust uppermost in his mind.*

In *Lovers and Liars* there is the incestuous abuse of Emily Ramsden by her uncle, Clem Jackson, out of which a girl, Cathleen, is born. But Clem is not the only wicked uncle in Jo's books. Caleb Crowther of the Emma Grady trilogy – *Outcast*, *Alley Urchin* and *Vagabonds* – is another. Both are based on a real-life uncle, described by Jo as 'the most evil man on earth: I hated him with a passion. He is the one Emma is terrified of. He is very cruel in that story, but it's just a reflection of how he was in real life. He was an uncle on my father's side, really a cousin but way older than us children and a nasty, devious, sly piece of work. We were quite frightened of him. When he turned up we would run and hide. He was very weird. I have always had this picture in my mind of him. I remember years later, twenty years ago, my husband Ken and I went to Blackburn, mainly to see family. We were driving along and I saw this uncle walking down the street and I went cold all over; that's how frightened I was of him. He had these searching eyes that looked right through you, rarely smiled, spooky.'

For Jo, family relationships are her priority. The loss of her own father and brothers after her family split becomes a driving force in her novels, perhaps explaining why abuse of the most blessed of relationships – family relationships – possesses her still.

It seems incredible that almost all the relationships in Jo's thirty-four novels are based on her own experience or the experience of someone close to her. 'Incest is to do with the fact that people did live so close together,' she agrees. 'I never had any experience of it, but somehow you knew things like that were going on. . . . There was a man who used to sell newspapers on Blackburn Boulevard and he had a daughter who was a little bit mentally retarded, and she had a baby and soon after that his wife left him and took the daughter and her baby with her, and there was talk. I heard the women talk.'

The women who figured in Jo's childhood were generally confined by unwritten laws to unrewarding domesticity in 'the old narrow houses with their steep unhygienic backyards, pot-sinks and outside lavvies. They experienced few luxuries, accepting hard work and domineering husbands as part of their unenviable lot,' she wrote in *Her Father's Sins*. Few even allowed themselves the luxury of self-pity or 'foolish dreams of what could never be'.

Into this forbidding picture the author introduces light brush-strokes of character that humanise and transform the community into one where Beth Ward (in *Don't Cry Alone*) finds 'another kind of love, a deep sense of belonging'. All-embracing mother figures abound. In *Somewhere, Someday* we have the warm, ebullient Lancashire landlady, Fran Docherty – 'a big, bustling mound of a woman, she had a soft, squashy smile that reminded Kelly of a newly stuffed eiderdown,' and in *Her Father's Sins*, besides Auntie Biddy, who is based on the author's own mother, Jo gives us Katy, who 'became the mother Queenie had never known but always craved.'

Jo was an unusually imaginative child. She has described herself as 'a people watcher' from the age of four. She needed the sanctuary of her imagination simply to survive, and always loved sharing her stories, even copping the odd pennies for the gas meter by telling made-up stories to friends amidst the rubble of bombed-out Blackburn town. The novels are littered with examples of imaginative observation – like Mr Eddie's long-johns 'squirming

15

half in half out' of Biddy's mangle, or like Mrs Aspen's box, used to stand on so that she can gossip with Biddy across the backyard wall.

The working-class community in Blackburn comes to us as a woven tapestry of relationships which represents every emotional facet of human life, the idiosyncratic ways of Jo's characters so often proving them true. We have tradesmen like old Dubber Butterfield who'd sit 'on his three-legged stool amidst the hundreds of boots, shoes and clogs which hung from the walls and ceilings', and Teddy, a 'twisted dwarf figure with huge pink eyes and a bald head', who runs a milk bar offering everything from a cure for toe-ache to a glass of sarsaparilla. Tales of schooldays and truancy bring us old Snake-tongue Jackson of St Mary's, and elsewhere in *Her Father's Sins* the old world is fingered in characters like Miss Tilly and Fancy Carruthers.

Then there is Maisie Thorogood, loose with the Yanks during the war and a rag-a-bone lady now, uproarious, louche, but, like Queenie's Aunt Biddy, at one with her environment. There is, indeed, no distinction – Maisie is her environment (as indeed are all Jo's characters): 'She'd always been part of it, like the gas-lamps and the shiny worn cobblestones.' Character, it seems, is not forged in response to the regime of life, it is one aspect of the environmental bedrock.

*   *   *

In her teens, when Jo's parents separated she moved south to Bedfordshire with her mother and sisters. At fifteen years of age she met her future husband, Ken, and they were married a year later. Her father, who had decried her efforts at writing and would be amazed to discover that she is the bestselling British women's author writing today, cut his daughter to the heart by refusing to give her away. By the time she came to write her first novel (published in 1987) she had long been an exile from her native Blackburn.

Her writing brought her back to her roots. It shocks us with its descriptions of poverty and fears of alcohol-induced violence, but at the same time it puts us in touch with the sense of belonging that underscored everything Jo held true in her childhood, a sense largely missing today in a world where community is too often merely a function of the Internet.

Both sides of Jo's childhood experience – the dark and the light – can be seen to be rooted in the extraordinary revolution that was enacted in Blackburn from the late eighteenth century, while the traumatic nature of her uprooting from the town in 1955 ensured that everything that has happened since continues to find imaginative reference in it.

CHAPTER ONE

The Web of Life

'Everything I have touched in my life figures in my books. Every single book I write has something that has happened to me or my family or to my friends.'

'I was born in Derwent Street in Blackburn, Lancashire, during the Second World War, and my earliest memories are of sitting on the front doorstep, watching the world being created in that street. I would see kids playing, men fighting, sweethearts having a tiff and then making up, and I'd just sit and stare at them, soaking it all in. If I close my eyes now I can still see it, just as if I were that five-year-old again. All the stories I have ever written have come from those people.'

The street was long, but straight like the lines of a railway track, lit by the tall blue-framed gas-lamps, which winked and sparkled at regular intervals on either side. From No. 2, which was right at the neck of the street, a body could look along the continuous row of tightly packed houses and experience the same sensation as if standing at the mouth of a long meandering tunnel.

The world that met Josephine Cox's curious stare from the doorstep of her house in the working-class Blackburn community of the 1940s was, as she noted in her first novel, *Her Father's Sins* (quoted above) – 'the old Lancashire, steeped in a tradition of cotton and ale':

A Lancashire unwelcoming and unresponsive to the gentle nudging wind of change ... Change would come, of that there could be no doubt. The old narrow houses with their steep unhygienic backyards, pot-sinks and outside lavvies, they wouldn't escape ... But for now, Auntie Biddy's Blackburn remained relatively intact and contented and fiercely defended by every man, woman and child, who had never experienced any other way. They delighted in the open-topped rattling trams, the muffin-man's familiar shout, as he pushed his deep wicker basket along the uneven cobbles, and the screech of the cotton-mill siren, starting another day. As long as one and all were left

*alone to make their own way, they bothered
nobody and asked no favours. The children
spilled out to all the streets, played with their
skipping-ropes, hula-hoops and spinning tops,
their laughter no less spontaneous because of
inherent poverty . . .*

Her Father's Sins is about the way things were: the
good times, the bad times. It is richly autobiographical. Queenie is the name of the little girl who experiences so many of the joys and traumas of Jo's early
life on the streets of Blackburn. Although her home
is transferred from Derwent Street to Parkinson
Street in the novel, they are, with reference to Jo's
early life, interchangeable.

*Lying in the half-dark, Queenie found it hard
to settle. She sensed something was wrong. But
what? After a while she dismissed the notion,
and turned over to warm Auntie Biddy's side of
the bed. But the uneasiness within her persisted.
And slipping out from underneath the persuasive warmth of the eiderdown, she crossed to
the window. For a change Parkinson Street was
all quiet, save for the pitiful mewing of a frustrated tom cat, and the occasional dustbin-
lid clattering to the flagstones beneath some
scampering cat's feet.
Queenie looked along the higgledy-piggledy*

21

Victorian sky-line. The irregular pattern of chimneys reaching up like the fingers of a deformed hand traced a weird but comfortingly familiar silhouette against the moonlit sky. Lifting the window up against the sash, Queenie leaned out so she had an unobstructed view of the street below. Parkinson Street was home: No. 2, Parkinson Street, and Auntie Biddy, they were hers, her comforting world into which she could retreat when things became complicated and painful.

'I loved the streetlamps and the cobbles,' Jo remembers of her earliest childhood. 'Many was the time I counted the cobbles in our street. When I had counted them from one end to the other, I counted the fanlights, the stained glass, on the way back. I had Queenie doing that.'

There were one hundred and four houses – Queenie had counted them all with loving precision. And there were one thousand and forty flagstones; Queenie had hopscotched every single one. She hadn't finished counting the road-cobbles yet, but up to Widow Hargreaves at No. 16, there were nine hundred and ten; that was counting across the road to the opposite houses. When she'd finished them, she would start on the stained glasses in the fanlight above the doors. Queenie meant to learn all there was to know about Parkinson Street because the more she knew, the more it was hers.

Stretching her neck, now, Queenie attempted to identify the dark figure approaching against the flickering gas-lamps. The tottering speck grew and grew, until it shaped itself into the towering frame of George Kenney. On recognising it, Queenie involuntarily backed away . . .

Though Derwent Street is gone, Parkinson Street, the imaginative theatre of Jo's real childhood joys and fears, still exists today and sparks characterful childhood memories of its own, Mill Hill being where some members of Jo's family settled after Jo's mum moved out in 1955. 'We had relatives there: Auntie Margaret lived up there and we'd go and see her. My brother, Bernard, lived for many years in Stephen Street. And another brother, Richard, lived on Parkinson Street, so we were always up there. I love that area of old Mill Hill, and I have set a lot of my stories there. It has changed now obviously – you've got the Indian takeaway and all that; they weren't there, it was just little shops and little houses and cobbled streets, and I loved it.'

Mill Hill, to the southwest of the town centre, developed in the latter part of the nineteenth century around Cardwell and Albert mills between the railway and the canal, together with another worker colony around Waterfall Mill in this same area, close to Parkinson Street.

The area may have seen change since Jo's childhood, but it is easy enough even today to catch a glimpse of how it was. The Navigation pub is still to be found by the bridge over the canal where Emma Grady's daughter, Molly, escapes from a prison van in *Alley Urchin*, although it has recently undergone a makeover. 'It's so old,' agrees Jo, 'and it's got the wooden benches around the wall and the real old characters, and my God you pick up some tales.'

She reminds me that the Navigation became her dad's haunt, and it is of course also George Kenney's local in *Her Father's Sins*, and in the *Outcast* trilogy (*Outcast, Alley Urchin* and *Vagabonds*), set in the second half of the nineteenth century, the pub is a haven for pickpockets and ruffians, and the place where Sal Tanner mistakes the attentions of a fellow in a spotted scarf for an invitation to bed.

> ''Ere . . . d'yer have a fancy for me?' Sal said in a low, excited voice. 'Got an urge ter tek me ter bed, have yer?' It was ages since any man had laid her down, and the thought of a tumble had her all excited. 'It'll cost yer a bit more than one gill though, me darlin',' she finished with a chuckle and a suggestive wink.

'Don't be so bloody daft, woman!' The poor fellow was shocked. 'I'm offering you a drink … Whatever gave you the idea that I'd want to take an old soak like you to bed?'

Old Sal, a legend in the area, 'a limping, bedraggled woman with thin, tousled hair and a kindly face that was ravaged by a rough life and a particular love for "a drop o' the ol' stuff"', was modelled on a woman who used to live down on the banks of the canal in a shed, an old hut between the pub and a vicarage. 'All the kids used to go and see her,' Jo told me.

The hut which was now home to Sal and Molly was situated at the widest area of grassy bank, and was half hidden in the undergrowth. There was a tall stone wall immediately behind, and directly behind that, the vicarage. This fact had given old Sal a great deal of pleasure as she told one and all: 'What more could a body want, eh? … I've got the ale house down one end, and the vicar at the other. If I'm tekken bad after a jolly night out, I have only ter whistle and the vicar'll come a'runnin' with his Bible. He'll get me ter the gates o' Heaven right enough. Drunk or sober, the good Lord won't turn me away, I'm thinking!'

When they had first come across the dilapidated workmen's hut, there were chinks

between the weathered boarding 'wide enough
ter drive a horse and cart through', as Sal had
complained. Now, however, the chinks were
stuffed with moss which Molly had painstak-
ingly gathered, and the wind couldn't force its
way in so easily. On a hot day like today,
though, the air inside the cramped hut was
stifling. 'Bloody hell, lass . . . prop that door
open with some'at!' instructed Sal as she fell
on to the narrow bed, this being a scrounged
mattress set on four orange-boxes, the whole
length of which swayed and creaked beneath
Sal's sudden weight.

'You'd walk to the pub with her and she'd sit you
on the step. And you'd hear all this noise going on
in the pub and I used to stand on tiptoes and look
through the window, and there was Sal on the counter, dancing, drunk as a lord, showing her knickers
to all and sundry. She was wonderful!' Jo put the
scene in *Outcast*:

Not daring to set foot in such a place, Emma
stood on tiptoe in order to look through the
windows. Her vision was impaired by the
frosted pattern on the glass and the large words
which read 'Public Bar' on the first window
and 'Snug' on the second. Peering through a
small corner below, where there was an area of

26

clear glass, Emma's view was still frustrated by the thick smoke screen and the wall of bodies inside . . . Suddenly a cackle of laughter erupted from within and as Emma peered through the haze in search of her husband, the unmistakable figure of Sal Tanner rose before her. The next moment, the laughing figure was hoisted on to one of the tables by a bevy of reaching, grasping hands. The music took on a more urgent note and the hands all began clapping as Sal Tanner executed a frenzied dance – showing her pink, grinning gums at one end and her pink, dimpled thighs at the other.

Soon after meeting Jo it became apparent just how completely the novels are based on her own personal experiences – not just the places, but the people, too, though this may be subtly done, so that, for example, Jo's real Auntie Biddy, who lived in Bedfordshire, was a quite different character to the one portrayed as the mother figure in *Her Father's Sins*. Only her name is used. Biddy's fictional character is in fact that of the author's mother, Mary Jane, who was the fulcrum of Jo's existence as a child, and in a sense remains so to this day: 'My mother was a lovely person. She was shy, but a very lovely looking lady – long dark hair, big dark eyes. She was ever so warm, you could never fall out with her.'

It was Jo's mum who encouraged her to realise

her ambition to become a writer, when the prospect seemed absurd. 'Sadly I didn't have success with the novels when she was alive, but she's up there, she knows . . . She is Marcia in *Angels Cry Sometimes*, and I keep her alive in each new novel. She's always there, sometimes she's an old woman, sometimes a young man . . . I had to keep her alive, you see. Molly Davidson was also my mother [*Cradle of Thorns*]. Marcia is most like her, but she appears in every novel. She could be an old man, a young woman, a little boy – the persona, the soul of that character is my mother. My readers are beginning to guess: "That is your mother!" In fact, reading the book I am writing now [*The Woman Who Left*], they might think that the female character, Georgie, is my mother, but they'll be fooled if they do, because it is someone who comes into the story later on . . .'

When I ask Jo what she particularly remembers about her mum, it is the simple things, how well they got on, the special, private, one-to-one moments of spontaneous laughter. Any one of the stories she tells me is typical: 'I remember once we were in the scullery and me mam said to me, "Take the potato peelings out of that water in that bowl, put them in the bucket there and swill the yard with the water." You had to go down a flight of steps to the backyard and as you came off the steps at the bottom you'd go into the smallest cellar, where the toilet was, and all the coal was kept in there. After telling me to do this, she went out, and I didn't know where she'd gone. So, anyway, I did what she said, took the potato peelings out of the bowl and put them in the bucket – we used to give them to the milkman who'd take them to the farm to feed to the pigs. Then I took the bowl of water and opened the back door and stood at the top of the steps and I just threw it. At that precise moment me mam came out of the toilet cellar and it went all over her! I thought I'd killed her! I cried my eyes out, and then of course we just laughed and laughed together. Just things like that, so lovely.'

Jo's dad, Barney Brindle, hailed from Kilkenny in southeast Ireland and had a job with the council when she was a child. 'He had these beautiful blue eyes and he was fair-haired, this little man, and I loved him very much,' said Jo. 'He worked for the Corporation on various jobs; he kept the roads, maintenance jobs, everything. Later, he kept Blackburn Rovers football ground, which he was immensely proud of. He was fanatical about Blackburn Rovers. Oh, my dad and my brothers were fanatical. And I loved it. I used to play football in the street and I've got a scar to prove it! See that scar? I dived for the ball and slit my left hand on some glass.

'Like the rest, my father worked extremely long hours. They had to because they had all these children. I mean, many of the families down the street had lots of children. So, the mothers were busy having the children and the men had to work to provide, and come the Friday they were worn out; they headed for the pub with the wages. It was a vicious circle.'

When Barney first met her mum, Mary Jane, in the 1930s, he was working as a quarryman and she was in her early twenties, lodging with her parents, Granddad and Grandma Harrison. Jo remembers her maternal grandparents well. They lived in Henry Street, Church, a suburb of Accrington, a town just east of Blackburn. Grandma Harrison is Grandma Fletcher in *Angels Cry Sometimes* – 'bossy, cantankerous, but with a heart of gold . . . I remember her old mangle, sitting in the yard through all weathers until Monday morning when it came alive at the turn of a handle.' And Jo remembers her grandpa as the one who opened her eyes to the magic of storytelling, when he sat her on his knee and told her stories of his adventures with his dog. Seventy-three-year-old Jasper Hardcastle in Jo's recent novel, *The Beachcomber*, 'was partly based on my granddad Harrison, a wonderful man, very special,' Jo admits. 'I remember one Sunday morning when I visited my beloved grandparents, I was eight years old and asked why the pan lid was dancing up and down on the stove. My granddad, who worked in the butcher's and used to get titbits at the end of the week, proudly lifted me up to show me a full pig's head boiling away in the pan, with the lid bobbing up and down on its ears! I ran screaming from the house, and it took them a full hour to get me out of the backyard loo.'

Jo learned all about her parents meeting from her mum, and the story became an essential part of the background to her third novel.

'*Angels Cry Sometimes* takes onboard a great deal of my mam's life,' Jo recently told the nation on BBC Radio 4's *Desert Island Discs*. 'When she was eighteen she was married to a man [before Jo's father] who made her life a misery. She was in love with this man. He married her. They had two little boys. And then about four years down the line the police came knocking at the door one day and they arrested him for bigamously marrying her and he was jailed for seven years.'

Readers will recognise this as the way Marcia Bendall's marriage to Curt Rathcter breaks down in the novel, even to the number of years that Curt is sentenced to serve at Lancaster Assizes:

When Curt came to the doorway of the little parlour, the policeman close behind, what he saw in there tore his heart to shreds. Seated on that very settee where many a time he and his darling Marcia had experienced so many tender and wonderful moments, was that same woman whom he idolised ... It gave Curt the deepest pain he had ever known when, at that moment, Marcia sensed his presence, for of a sudden she raised her large dark eyes to look on him. Their painfully stricken expression made him ask silently for the Lord's forgiveness.

On seeing him there also, both the officer and Grandma Fletcher got up from their seats. He asked whether the fellow's name was Curt Ratheter. She charged forward and angrily demanded of him, 'Is it true what they're saying? 'Ave yer already a wife?'

'My mother wouldn't talk about it for a long, long time because it was such a stigma,' Jo told me. 'Suddenly she was an unmarried mother and he was in prison. It made her life a misery. I think she must have still been in love with him when he was taken away. He moved south when he came out. Then she met Dad, Barney. He was a happy-go-lucky chap, up for a laugh, charming as ever. And he loved her very much. And she grew to love him.'

With such a background to a marriage, successful as it was in one sense, with ten of Barney's children born to Mary over the next two decades, it cannot ever have been easy for Jo's dad to accept that it had only been made possible through a breach of the law. Did Barney know that his new wife still loved this man who had been put in prison? Did that count in the sad balance of fate that led Jo to say on BBC Radio: 'They had lots and lots of children, and I am obviously one of them, but along the way, somewhere, they started to bring out the worst in each other'?

Whether or not it did, there are plenty of other reasons that would count against the marriage surviving, to be found in the difficult environment in which the young family was immediately thrown.

In the fiction, Barty Bendall (who is Barney Brindle, Jo's father) begs Marcia to marry him and give her and Ratheter's children a father. When, finally, she consents, they marry and move to Blackburn, just as in reality Barney and Mary Jane did.

Derwent Street, their first home, had been fields until the second half of the nineteenth century, when it emerged as part of the dense concentration of mill workers' terraced rows into which Jo was born. It was a very poor area, all to be torn down a century later. Ruby Miller lives there in Jo's novel *Nobody's Darling*. Mollie and her fiancé, Alfie, try for a house there in *Looking Back*. In *Rainbow Days*, 'the ruined house at the bottom of Derwent Street was a favourite meeting place for villains,' and in *The Woman Who Left* it is the place to which Sal, Louise and Ben Hunter must return when they are stripped of beautiful Maple Farm on the outskirts of the town. Louise gives her true feelings: 'I often stand at that front window and look down Derwent Street, and my heart sinks to me boots.' Jo's message is clear: you can't fall much lower than Derwent Street.

However, for an imaginative child born in the summer of 1941, during the Second World War, a child who knew nothing of the wider world, Derwent Street was all-consuming. The street 'was all little houses,' Jo told me, 'but it was a real community. The house was heated by a coal fire, if you were lucky enough to have any coal. There was a tiny scullery, no bigger than a few feet. Back parlour, front parlour, each of the parlours had a tiny fire grate.' The scullery appears in *Take This Woman* – 'a cold, forbidding place, separated from the parlour by a heavy brown curtain at the door-way. It was some eight feet square, consisting of an old gas-cooker, a single wooden cupboard with several shelves above it, and a deep stone sink beneath the window. Built into the corner was a brick container, housing a copper washtub and closed at the top by a large circular lid of wooden slatted design.'

To this came Barney and Mary Jane Brindle, and Mary's two children by her first marriage, the family swelling in time to include, besides Jo, her two sisters, Winifred and Anita, and seven brothers: Sonny (so named because as a child he was always smiling), Joseph, Bernard, Richard, Billy, Harry and Alec.

Like Amy Tattersall with her brood in *Looking Back*, the Brindles suffered the trials of so many growing up in a cramped house:

'My earliest memories . . . sitting on the front doorstep, watching . . .'

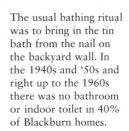

The usual bathing ritual was to bring in the tin bath from the nail on the backyard wall. In the 1940s and '50s and right up to the 1960s there was no bathroom or indoor toilet in 40% of Blackburn homes.

'I am very aware of how it used to be. Inside I haven't changed a bit. I am still that snotty-nosed kid from the back streets.'

Above: Blackburn, Josephine Cox's birthplace in the 1950s, when there were 200 factory chimneys scraping the sky and the soot was said to blacken the fleece of sheep on the Pennine Hills 15 miles away.

Below: 'The tall mill chimneys belched out their fumes and the grey-black vapour settled like a dark cloud over the whole town, blotting out the sun and filling the air with specks of charcoal that irritated the throat and stung the eyes...' *Jessica's Girl*

Derwent Street, the street where Jo Cox was born, was like any other, 'a narrow, cobbled street with tightly packed rows of thin grubby doors that opened straight out onto the pavement, it was noisy, dirty, swarming with people, but wonderfully welcoming. The women, laughing or talking, and nearly all pregnant, were busy white-stoning the steps, washing the windows, or watching young 'uns, who spent their days sitting on the kerbs with sugar butties; sailing matchstick boats down the gutters; and dropping loose stones into the stinking drains.' *Take This Woman*

'It was a little house we had in Derwent Street,' Jo remembers, 'they were all little houses, but it was a real community.'

Belonging to a place, to a street, to a people, to a family 'is the most important thing,' says Jo. 'That "sense of belonging" is you, it is who you are, it is where you came from.'

The Blackburn Ragged School, one of a system originally devised, wrote Charles Dickens, for those 'who are too ragged, wretched, filthy and forlorn, to enter any other place: who could gain admission into no charity-school, and who would be driven from any church door.' Jo Cox attended this one from the age of four till nine.

Blackburn Union Workhouse had become Queen's Park Hospital before Jo was born, but outside relief was still available for the needy at Nazareth House, a Catholic Convent and sanctuary. 'The sisters would feed us and give me mam a few bob,' Jo recalls.

Cicely Bridge Mill, the cotton mill where Jo's mum worked.

'I remember going in to the mill for the first time and I couldn't believe how hard me mam had to work. They all wore aprons with big pockets. The noise was horrendous! Huge machines, great big rooms.'

August 1940, the second bombing raid on Blackburn, and the second in twenty-four hours.

'I started charging the kids a penny each to sit on the bomb rubble while I told them stories. If any didn't have a penny, I'd kick 'em out,' Jo recalls.

'There was a lot of laughter and we made our own fun, but the hardship was always there,' says Jo. 'You are not supposed to suffer when you are a child, but at home there was never food in the cupboards. Only when I went to proper school did I realise we were really poor, that I was different from other people living in better streets.'

'Four little 'uns and the two older girls. Six altogether.' She rolled her eyes. *'Might as well be sixty, the way they drive me to despair.'*

Horrified, and unable to take his eyes off the army of children, he asked, *'How do you manage?'*

'I get by.' She laughed. *'I don't know how Frank will cope though, when this one arrives in a month's time. He doesn't know one from the other as it is!'*

'At one stage we slept six in a bed in an attic room – three top, three bottom,' Jo recalls. 'We had a couple of blankets and my dad's khaki overcoat thrown over us. The lavatory was outside and the walls were paper thin . . . You'd get someone's foot in your mouth when you were half-asleep. But it was part of the normality of life . . . Like any family, ours has its ups and downs, its joys and sorrows, but beneath all of that is a great reservoir of love, and to this day we always watch out for each other.'

In between having her many children, and right through her pregnancies, Jo's mum worked in the carding room of Cicely Bridge Mill, preparing the cotton fibres for spinning. Tucked behind the railway station on the south bank of the Leeds–Liverpool canal, Cicely Bridge Mill specialised in spinning, while, opposite, Alma Mill specialised in weaving.

'The knocker-up used to wake me dad up to go

to work, used to wake the whole house up, actually,' recalls Jo. 'It was a long stick knocking on the [upper] windows, still going on in the early 1950s. Every day started the same noisy, predictable way: bleary-eyed workers tumbling from their beds, the screech of the factory hooters, droves of blue overalls, flat caps and khaki demob-coats, billy-cans a-rattling and snap-tins shaping their deep pockets.' Jo describes the scene in *Jessica's Girl* and *Angels Cry Sometimes*:

The market-hall clock was showing sixthirty... Already the town was awake. Hordes of cotton mill workers huddled together, pushing towards Cicely Bridge, their flat caps like a sea of twill and their snap-cans clinking in rhythm with the stamp of their ironrimmed clogs on the pavements ... The tram shuddered to a halt, jerking Marcia's wandering thoughts to the long hard day ahead at the spinning frames. The bleary-eyed workers, tired and worn even before they started, tumbled from the tram, all pushing and shoving towards their place of labour. 'Morning Marcia lass ...' 'Bit parky, eh ... shouldn't send a dog out this time o' the day!' 'Ow do, Marcia love; weekend coming up, eh ... thank Christ!'

The muffled-up workers shouted their cheery greetings, as they hunched their shoulders

against the piercing cold, and set about trudg-
ing their way up Cicely to the sprawling cluster
of cotton mills there. Marcia returned their
friendly greeting with genuine affection . . .

As the hurrying throng of mill-hands
swarmed across the top of Cicely Hill to dis-
perse along various paths leading to their re-
spective mills, the sounds of their departing
voices was effectively silenced beneath the
banshee wail of the five-minute hooter.

'Come on, Marcia! You shoulda done your
dreaming while you were still abed! Or
wouldn't the old fella let you, eh?'

Marcia turned at the coarse laughter which
cut through her private thoughts. 'Oh, morning
Old Fred,' she said as she stopped for the
merest second to rub her hands in the intensity
of heat radiating from the brazier. Old Fred
was the night-watchman, a harmless little man
with a mountain of cheek and more than his
fair share of smutty humour . . .

Jo remembers old Fred very well: 'Harmless, but
incredibly ugly. Whenever I went up to Cicely Bridge,
he was the little man always sitting there. "All right,
lass?" he'd ask. He didn't talk a lot, in fact, he was
just a funny little creature sitting there.

'I remember going into the mill for the first time
and I couldn't believe how hard me mam had to

work. They all wore aprons with big pockets. The noise was horrendous! Huge machines, great big rooms.

'And do you know they had their own language? They couldn't hear what was being said, so they had their own language. It wasn't a sign language with fingers but with the mouth. They used their mouths. My mum could talk to someone right at the other end, and they could converse, they knew what each of them was saying. You couldn't hear a thing.'

The most crippling discomfort, and the hardest to get used to, was the noise. The constant high-pitched whine from the machines, tempered with a rhythmic thumping, was painfully deafening and nerve-jarring. In the monstrous Victorian building which swallowed Marcia's days, the spinning and weaving machines dominated thought and action. It was physically impossible for the workers to converse in an easy normal manner. Pitching the mere human voice against the brawling of these tireless machines was utterly futile. So, in the deviousness born of necessity, the Lancashire millhands had devised a silent but functional language of their own. With their sophisticated sign- and lip-reading language they cheated the screaming machines which sought to render them mute.

Marcia's clocking-in card was the last in the rack. Everyone had punched their cards and placed them in the in-shelves. She slipped the yellow card into the slot over the time-clock, just as the hand swung round to register six a.m. 'Good,' she whispered, tapping the clock gratefully, 'just in time!'

As she pushed against the heavy green doors leading into the cloakroom, she could hear the machines starting up one after the other. Wriggling out of her coat, she slung it hurriedly over one of the pegs on the rack before hastening to her own machine.

'Come on, Marcia! Where the 'ell 'ave you been?' Tom Atkinson was the gaffer. A great elephant of a man he was; shaped like one of the cotton-bobbins, swollen to bulging in the middle and tapered off at both ends. His watery red-rimmed eyes were incapable of direct focus because while the left one struggled to hold you tight in its quivering gaze, the right one swivelled about all over the place, until finally out of utter frustration the pair of them gave up the effort . . .

Without uncovering her long black hair, she skilfully manipulated the scarf about her head, transforming it into a knotted turban which sat tight and snug, concealing and protecting her magnificent hair from the clinging wisps of cotton which would soon fill the air like sticky snowflakes. Reaching into a small wooden locker beneath her bobbin-crate, she exchanged her ankle-clogs for soft slippers. Then she donned the regular green wrap-around overall. Strapping the deep-pocketed pinny around her waist, and checking the bottom tray-run to assure herself that it was filled all the way along with empty bobbins, Marcia threw the machine into gear. Marcia wasn't normally given to nervousness, but the act of triggering the monstrous machine into life was definitely not one in which she took pleasure.

'Tom Atkinson, the gaffer. I remember him. He was a man of few words, in charge of my mother's section. He didn't like children. He didn't speak to me. He was just someone that was there who was part of what was going on in my mother's life, you know?

'But Big Bertha was the woman who worked on the next lot of machines from my mum. The one thing I remember about her was that she had this big round face and was always laughin'!

'Often, at the end of the day, I would walk up to Cicely Bridge and meet me mam,' Jo remembers. 'I pushed the little babbies in the pram to meet her. I was only about nine meself. I would sit waiting for her, sit on a stool at the bottom of the run. I can see her now: at the end of each run of machine they would have a box and they would keep their slippers in there, and these slippers were the funniest things because they were just like big clumps of snow, where all the cotton had settled on them, month after month. The cotton, it would fall like snow and you'd be covered in it in five seconds, and the slippers just grew, and they shoved their feet into these great things and ran up and down the row of bobbins. She had eight bobbins to look after . . .'

These were the bobbins that received the slender rope or 'roving' of spun cotton fibres in the mechanised pre-spinning process, described in my *Introduction*. 'Me mam had to keep putting the empty bobbins on and taking the full ones off, dropping them in her apron,' said Jo. 'And if you weren't quick then it'd spill over and you'd be in a dreadful mess. They worked like this from six in the morning till six at night, all the time running up and down . . .'

The cotton poured out in great abundance, winding and wrapping itself around the receptive bobbins which spun and twirled, until swollen pregnantly with their heavy load. When full, the heavy bobbins would be removed by the harassed scurrying women who constantly raced against time and machine as they darted methodically from one end of the heaving row to the other, their coloured

41

turbans making frenzied patterns as they wove up and down, up and down.

The frequent replacement of empty bobbins for full ones was swift and skilful. The empty bobbins were quickly dropped with great accuracy over the fast spinning core-rods. It took only a few minutes for the empty bobbins to fill to bursting again; allowing the constantly mobile women no rest. They were hard pushed to keep up, and many a trainee had surrendered in tears to the devouring machines. The full bobbins were slipped into the hessian bag which the women wore around their waists until the bag reached overflowing. The bobbins were then emptied into large square wicker containers. These, in turn, were emptied into huge mobile trollies, which were frequently transported to another level of the mill by an organised army of 'trundlers'. The fine cotton would then be woven into endless acres of fresh crisp linen, to be shipped all over the world, as well as marketed locally.

'Do you remember the man in the novel who used to take the trolleys and the women scragged him?' Jo asked me. 'Well, my mam told me about this man, Tommy Trindle, who took the full bobbin trolleys away and brought the empty trolleys back, and he was always pinching their bottoms and making snide little comments, so they did scrag him one day. They got his trousers off and shoved him down the ramp in the trolley!'

George Leatherhead was a 'trundler' who took a pride in his work . . . Unfortunately for poor George, some of the young flighty girls, always ready for a bit of fun at the end of a working day, had overheard his brazen remarks. He didn't get very far before they were on him, their pent-up exuberance now released in fits of screaming laughter.

'Right, you sexy beast, George Leatherhead! You've asked for it now!' 'Don't get worriting, George . . . we're not going to 'arm you . . . we just want to see what all the fuss is about.' 'Come on, George! Get them bloody trousers off!' They came at him from all directions . . .

Stories like this leave little doubt about the camaraderie that relieved the twelve-hour work shifts until the factory hooter blew for shutdown and the spinning machines were wound down. Bit by bit the blanket of noise broke up and dissipated, as one by one the individual sources of it were extinguished. Normally a swell of laughter and chatter would replace the machine noise, but on one occasion, Jo tells me, there was only hushed silence. 'That terrible scene in *Angels Cry Sometimes* is based on something

43

that one of the ladies who worked with Mam told
me when she took me to the toilet . . . She was telling
me about this girl . . . and then, "Don't you go near
the machines, lass," she said . . .':

*'Come on, Marcia! Get your apron emptied!'
But even as Marcia was lifting her hand to
throw the switch which would close down her
machine, there came an almighty noise from
some way up in front – a great screeching, jar-
ring noise, which was unlike anything she'd
heard before. Then, of a sudden, it was like all
hell let loose! Folks ran in all directions and
even Tom Atkinson, who judging by the heightened colour of his face and the wild look in
his eyes, could go down any minute with a
heart-attack, pelted past Marcia's machine.*

*By now most of the machines had ground
to a halt. But, when Marcia emerged from
changing her slippers for shoes, she saw little
groups of mill-hands standing about and con-
versing in whispers. From a distance, she could
see Daisy crying, with old Bertha comforting
her. Some of the other women were stark-eyed,
with their hands flattened over their mouths as
though to stifle any sound that might come out.*

*Going to where old Bertha had young Daisy
enclosed in her arms, Marcia asked in a soft
voice, subdued by the sight of wretched faces*

all about her, 'What is it, Bertha? Whatever's going on?'

But Bertha could give no answer, except to shake her head and gently to lead away the trembling girl in her arms. As she passed Marcia she whispered, 'Come away, lass. Come away!' As Marcia made to follow her . . . there came a flurry of activity from both behind and in front of her.

Tom Atkinson walked about, going from one little group to another, gently moving them on and telling them, 'Tek yersel's off home. There's nowt to be done 'ere!' His face looked totally drained of colour and his shoulders stooped as though pressed down with a great weight.

When the two dark-suited fellows came hurrying by her carrying a rolled-up stretcher and looking grim, Marcia's eyes followed them and, almost involuntarily, she took a few paces forward. What she saw came as one of the worst shocks she had ever experienced. It was Maggie Clegg's machine around which all activity was taking place – bright, chirpy Maggie Clegg's machine, splattered from top to bottom in great splashes of blood standing out scarlet and horrifying against the white cotton bobbins and the great iron struts, which Maggie knew like the back of her hand. From the huge cogs and rollers which ran this monstrosity, there hung ragged hanks of hair – Maggie's hair that was once long and jet-black, and which now was crimson and split asunder.

Jo's world is sometimes harsh, and when it is, the benefits of belonging to a community come into play. The character of her people *is* the environment from which the stories flow, so that, for example, Queenie's house draws from her mother's strong, loving character, and offers the little girl security:

There was a degree of warmth and splendid reliability in the stalwart green distemper, which reflected the half-light from the gas-lamp beneath the window. The big square wardrobe stood to attention in its disciplined uprightness, as it towered protectively over a short wooden-knobbed chest of drawers. A small ripple of pleasure bathed the knot of fear in Queenie's stomach as her gaze rested on the kidney-shaped dresser . . . There in the half-light were all the familiar things.

'It was a little house we had in Derwent Street,' Jo reminisces, 'they were all little houses, but it was a real community. You could go out and leave your door unlocked, then come back and find six people sitting in your kitchen drinking tea. The women all looked after each other's children. Nobody had much, but we shared what we had.'

'Belonging to a place, to a street, to a people, to a family is important to you,' I suggest.

'It is *the* most important thing,' Jo agrees. 'It is you, it is who you are, it is where you came from. I think every day of my life . . . I am very aware of how it used to be. Inside I haven't changed a bit. I am still that snotty-nosed kid from the backstreets. I have been more fortunate than a lot of people, but my feet are firmly on the ground. From Derwent Street come the really early memories, when I was four, five years old and I would sit on the step and watch everything as it was going on in the street.

'We were very poor and constantly moved house, but of all the places we lived I remember Derwent Street in particular. We had a chap who used to live at the top end, who dressed up in high heels and short skirts! All the children would follow him up and down the street as if he were the Pied Piper. And then he was arrested one day. The policemen were taking him off and we were all running after him! We all loved him! He was so kind, a lovely man.'

In *Her Father's Sins*, the cross-dresser appears in the guise of Fountain Crossland, 'who had fists the size of sledge-hammers and a head like a stud-bull, a burly pit worker', but who would rather be wearing Auntie Biddy's pinny and dandling Queenie on his knee.

It was a pleasing picture that greeted Fountain Crossland when George Kenney's daughter opened the door to his tapping. 'A sight for sore eyes, that's what you are, young Queenie,' he said quietly. Then without waiting to be asked he stepped inside and proceeded down the passageway towards the parlour. Queenie closed the door and followed. 'He's still in bed,' she said, leaving the parlour door open as she came in from the passage. 'No need fer that,' Fountain Crossland told her, his face crooked into a half-smile.

Queenie had already turned away with the intention of rousing George Kenney but now the big man came to block her exit. Putting his finger across his lips he leaned towards her, at the same time reaching out behind her to push the door to. 'Ssh . . . we don't want to fetch 'im from 'is bed, do we? I've seen what 'e's like on wakkening!' He stretched his face into an ugly grimace, and it was such an accurate mimicry of George Kenney in a foul temper that Queenie found herself laughing out loud in spite of herself. Auntie Biddy had no liking for Fountain Crossland, Queenie knew, but he could be so funny, and a great deal nicer than George Kenney.

'Auntie Biddy abed too is she?'

'Yes . . . she's been badly.'

'Ah! Works too 'ard does Biddy.' Fountain Crossland seated himself in the horse-chair by the fireside, all the while regarding Queenie through careful eyes. 'I'll tell you what, lass,' he said quietly, 'let's you an' me 'ave a little talk eh?' His broad smile was disarming, and when he stretched out a hand Queenie went to him.

At once he pulled her on to his knee and Queenie was quickly enthralled by the stories he told her . . . funny stories about little creatures who lived in folks' mattresses and who had the most marvellous adventures.

It seemed that Fountain Crossland got carried away in excitement, because once or twice Queenie found herself being violently jiggled up and down on his lap. And when at one stage Fountain Crossland took to acting out a scene where he took off his trousers and put on Auntie Biddy's pinafore he looked so silly that Queenie fell about laughing.

It was this scene that Auntie Biddy came upon when she brought herself down from the bedroom to investigate the noise. It took her but a moment to see Fountain Crossland's real game and with a cry of 'You fornicating old sod!' she grabbed up his trouser belt and whacked it hard across his bare legs. 'Out! Get out and don't show yourself here again!' she told him. Even when Fountain Crossland took to his heels and ran off up the passage without his trousers, Auntie Biddy would have followed him if it hadn't been for the fact that the bubble of energy she had summoned was now depleted. Falling into the nearest chair, she told the gaping Queenie, 'Throw 'is old trousers after him, lass.'

This Queenie did, firmly closing the front door after both Fountain Crossland and his trousers had disappeared through it, only to be tripped head over heels by Mrs Farraday's terrified ginger tom. When she returned to the parlour, Queenie was uncertain as to whether she would be blamed for letting Fountain Crossland into the house, and looked into the little woman's face with a sheepish expression.

'I'm sorry, Auntie Biddy,' Queenie said. For a moment there came no response. Then, just as Queenie began to think she would not be forgiven, she noticed a twinkle which spread into a smile and the smile erupted into laughter. Queenie ran to her Auntie Biddy and together the two of them rocked helplessly at the memory of Fountain Crossland fleeing up the passage in a pinny, after having his buttocks well and truly thrashed by Auntie Biddy.

There were other more or less permanent sentinels, too, like old Mr Craig from No. 46:

> *Queenie liked Mr Craig, who spent long lonely days sitting outside his little house. The rickety stand-chair had a permanent place on the flag-stones by the front door. Folks had long ago stopped asking questions or wondering why it was that a stand-chair should be left outside in all weathers year in year out. They'd gotten used to the old fellow sitting there, happy to pass the time of day with anyone who could spare it. From early morning to last thing at night when the biting chill of evening forced him in, he'd just sit there smiling and chatting to one and all, and generally watching the world go by.*
>
> *During her flag-counting sessions, Queenie would often run errands for him, or come and set herself on his step, where she'd listen enthralled to exciting stories of his daredevil days and frightening accounts of the war he'd fought in as a young man.*

'You have to love life and love people if you are going to write stories,' says Jo today. 'You must live the part of every character, even the bad ones. When I am writing I am laughing and crying, and feeling angry and sad. I have so many stories I would have to live to 200 to write them all.'

Time and again it is Jo's women who make the strongest characters: 'Ada Humble in *Angels Cry Sometimes* was my mam's friend, Mrs Brown. She was a fat little woman, a lovely, lovely person.' Ada is noted for her washing line and 'the numerous shirt-tails that pranced in the drying breeze, telling the world and its neighbour that she was the proud custodian of seven darling men.' The novels are littered with imaginative observations from the perspective of the curious little girl next door. More significant, however, was Ada's red trilby. 'She had a red trilby, and, do you know, she wore that trilby everywhere. She lived next door to us, and we would laugh when every morning she would come out and bend down to pick up the milk and her trilby would stay on! She never would be seen without that trilby.'

Ada Humble was only forty-one, but looked much older. She laid no great claims to beauty and her demands were few. The great sagging belly which always looked well-advanced in pregnancy had been stretched and shaped that way by the six strapping lads she'd borne her husband Toby Humble.

The podginess of her rosy cheeks gave her a cheery clownish appearance, emphasised by the vivid colour of her round eyes, which shone bright and brown, 'like a good strong brew of tea' Marcia had often observed. But the most surprising feature about her was the red broad-brimmed trilby, which had become her trade-mark. It had been white at one time. But after cadging it from the local muffin-man, in exchange for an old pair of pram wheels for his dilapidated wicker-trolley, Ada Humble had dipped it in a dye of her own making. The end result had not been the deep respectable plum colour she'd intended, but a screaming bright shade of tarty-red. It didn't deter Ada from wearing it though. There wasn't a living soul now who could ever remember Ada Humble without 'that trilby'.

'What happened to Ada was very sad,' Jo tells me. 'She had five sons. One of them wouldn't go to school. She used to come and tell my mam, and my mam said, "Take him in. Put him through the door. Make sure he gets into the classroom." Ada did this, but he would still run off and the truant officer kept coming round, and finally he said, "If the boy doesn't go to school, you'll have to go to Court." Ada was taken to court. My mam went with her.'

An uncomfortable silence settled over the court-room as the magistrate's thin bony face twisted itself into an expression of painful thought. Then calling the same man to attention, he asked in a sharp voice, 'May we ask the reason for the non-removal of Mrs Humble's head-piece?'

Marcia hadn't thought of that! She'd been so used to seeing that bright red trilby atop Ada Humble's head that it had become part of the little woman herself, yet by the tone of the magistrate's voice, he was pompous enough to consider its presence as a deliberate mark of disrespect.

'We would beg the court's pardon,' the young man returned, extending his apology to include a reminder of the recent death of Mr Humble, and of the accused's condition of mourning. 'It is meant in no way as an affront to the court or its proceedings.' But the magistrate was obviously not placated. In fact, judging by the sour expression on his face, and the sharp way he turned to consult his colleagues, Marcia felt almost as though Ada's red trilby had suddenly become the issue, and not Blackie's truancy.

'Poor thing, she was jailed, for six months!' says Jo. 'They decreed that Ada's husband [Toby] couldn't have been blamed because he had been at work, it wasn't his fault – he had been innocent of this – it was the mother at home's fault, so Ada was put in jail. When she came out she was broken! She had lost all her weight – she was like a stick! – she was white, she was haggard and she died soon after. It was terrible.

'Now, when somebody died, all the people in the street had to go along and pay their respects, and the children too. I said, "No." I didn't want to go. And I kicked and screamed. But my mam dragged us along, and there was little Ada in her coffin without her hat, and she was completely bald. That was why she had always worn the trilby! None of us had known. My mother saw the hat on the chair and she picked it up and put it on Ada's head. I'll never forget that.'

Now Marcia's gaze travelled along the gleaming chrome trellis which proudly bore the weight of that tiny, polished wood coffin. Of a sudden she was staring at the inner silk which lay ruffled over the little figure in white billowing folds, and slowly she reached out to touch the podgy fingers, folded in perpetual prayer. In the silence of that room the choking sob which caught in Marcia's throat seemed to startle even herself.

Crossing the still hands, she marvelled at their cold parchment beauty, then withdrawing her touch, she focused on the large cross on the wall over the head of the coffin, as though drawing strength to look again on Ada

Humble's face. The arch of flickering light from the half-circle of tiny candles which cradled the head of the coffin drew her eyes down, and her stricken gaze alighted on the ever-familiar lines of the little woman's face.

The bright red trilby – which Ada's insensitive ''fficials' had taken from her – Marcia had gently placed over the wispy stumps of hair and ragged bald patches which Ada Humble had managed to hide from the curious world for so long. It made a stark contrast against the soft silky whiteness of the pillow. As Marcia dwelt soulfully on the dear face, a sick fury tugged at her senses. Half seeing through the misty veil, she leaned forward to place a gentle kiss on the alabaster forehead. 'I know you'd not want yon town hall folk to tek your Toby – your "soldier",' she whispered, 'so you tek him, Ada lass, for he belongs to nobody else.' She removed the frame from around Toby's picture, then slid the rolled up picture gently underneath the long shroud and out of sight. Somehow, the act gave her a feeling of pleasure.

The inhabitants of working-class Blackburn were as varied and interesting as the higgledy-piggledy pattern of chimneys that formed its skyline, like old Martha Heigh, another eccentric of the street:

She could be seen now, standing on her door-step, stretching her neck so as not to miss any-thing. Martha Heigh never bothered to wash . . . or so it was told. Anyone, it was rumoured, with even half a nose could not bear to stand within range of the very nasty aroma which constantly surrounded old Martha.

She'd lived on her own in the last house along the row these thirty-odd years, since the death of her poor old father. Nobody knew her real age although folks reckoned it to be grander than eighty. She rarely ventured from the safety of her home, and the only person she had ever allowed inside it was Marcia who, to the horror of her neighbours, often fetched groceries for the old woman.

Martha was as short and round as a little Toby jug, and the full-length skirts she wore did nothing to enhance her appearance. More often than not, the skirt was employed as a convenient dish rag. She'd wipe her hands on it, blow her snuffy brown nostrils on it . . . she was using it now to shine up her precious tiny silver spectacles, which were then promptly placed on her nose with delicate precision as she peered to focus.

Her hair stood out in a petrified state of attention, and the nervous nodding habit she'd cultivated accelerated with excitement at the appearance of the new neighbours. The wide appreciative grin as she suddenly saw Marcia displayed the blackened rows of teeth, the naturalness of which she was duly proud. Marcia smiled back, waving her hand in acknowledgement.

Then there were the street traders – the peddler, the tinker with pots and pans, the scissors grinder and the barrel-organ grinder:

A little wizened man had placed his barrel organ in a shrewd position, so that anyone emerging from Ainsworth Street had no choice but to pass him before reaching the centre of activity.

'Good evening one an' all!' His voice was an odd grating squeak which seemed to suit his tiny size and general set-up. Fascinated at both his goblin-like appearance and the whole un-usual ensemble before them, the little party ground to a halt.

'Mam! Just look at that!' Polly's voice was tremulous with the eager excitement of a child. 'That's a monkey!' The incredulity in Polly's voice caused them to stare all the harder.

'That's right, lass. You're looking at the gamest little monkey in Lancashire!' The wiz-ened man stepped forward with the monkey

squatting skilfully on the bony protrusion of his shoulder and the light from a corner street-lamp illuminated the weird pair. Marcia couldn't help but notice the striking resemblance between the monkey and its shrunken owner. They were both of the same scrawny appearance, and even the cheeky red cap perched jauntily on the monkey's head was identical to the one worn by the man. 'I'm tellin' you,' he continued to squawk, 'there's no monkey in the whole of Lancashire – perhaps the whole world – as can do tricks like my Jasper 'ere!' He swung the monkey by the length of its confining lead to land with a soft thud on Polly's shoulder. His quick jerky movements startled her into springing forward, whereupon the monkey flew into the air, emitting a series of jabbering squawks and chatters, before landing squarely on the side of the barrel organ.

Pre-eminent amongst the street traders was, of course, the rag-and-bone merchant. *Take This Woman*, set in Blackburn in 1947, presents us with Laura Blake, who makes a canny living out of 'tatting', as it is known. She collected from a lumbering wooden cart, manoeuvring it by settling herself between its long curved shafts, and taking a firm grip with each hand. She'd collect from the smart area of town, along the Preston New Road, and then wend her way back towards Remmie Thorpe's rag-and-bone shop, where she might exchange some of what she had collected for a few shillings. But Laura found a better welcome in her own part of town, as this extract shows:

> *The women, all turbaned, laughing or talking, and nearly all pregnant, were busy white-stoning the steps, washing the windows, or watching young 'uns, who spent their days sitting on the kerbs with sugar butties; sailing matchstick boats down the gutters; and dropping loose stones into the stinking drains.*
>
> *'Hey up!' Smiling Tilly Shiner was the first to spot Laura and her cumbersome cart. 'It's young Laura!'*
>
> *'Tongue 'anging out for a brew, I expect.' The broad-faced Belle Strong waved a fat dimpled arm towards Laura. 'Get your arse into my kitchen, young 'un!' she shouted coarsely, her numerous chins waggling and bright round eyes laughing. 'Leave yon cart agin the kerb. They'll 'ave it filled in no time, lass!'*

And what does Tilly intend to give her? A pair of brown, iron-clad clogs. In *Her Father's Sins*, Jo recalls the occasion when, as a youngster, she took her dad's boots out to another rag-and-bone lady. Maisie Thorogood was as much part of the street scene 'as the gas-lamps and the shiny worn cobble-stones. In real life she was really quite bad, which was why I called her Thorogood in the book.' In the continuation of Queenie's story, *Let Loose the Tigers*, Maisie and her daughter, Sheila, are charged with keeping an immoral house in Lytham St Annes, and Sheila is sent to prison for five years. In real life, Maisie's great weakness concerned the Yanks. The American GIs came to the town in 1944. They arrived to prepare for the invasion of Europe and were accommodated in the then disused Brookhouse Mill. 'Maisie liked them a lot,' Jo's mother had informed her, 'and when the Yanks left, she was left behind with twins, called Raymond and Sheila in the book. I grew up with them.

'Maisie had connections with everything. She was amazing. She was wonderful! She was like fairyland! She had this cart that she had painted, and she attached balloons to it. You thought the whole thing was going to take off! You couldn't miss her. Big peroxide-blonde hair. A voice like a sergeant major. Great sense of humour. She'd have everyone in stitches. The men used to tease her and torment her and she'd give 'em as good as she got, swore like a trooper!'

Clutching George Kenney's old boots, Queenie hopped and skipped the few flagstones which separated her from the rag-a-bone wagon. Its presence within the excited screeching throng of children was pinpointed by the numerous clusters of waving balloons. Every colour of the rainbow they were, dancing and jiggling towards the sky in erratic fits and starts, as the ticklish breeze played and teased the restraining strings.

There were sausage-shaped ones, round ones, egg-shaped and twisty ones; all wriggling and singing as they rubbed together gleefully. Queenie had often imagined Maisie Thorogood sitting in her parlour blowing up the balloons. The magnitude of such an operation had prompted her on more than one occasion to ask Maisie where she kept all that wind, and if it took her all week to get the balloons ready. Maisie would roll about and scream with laughter. 'Bless your 'eart, Queenie darlin',' she'd shout, 'didn't you know I keeps a goblin in me shoe. It's 'im as blows 'em up!' So frustrated and perplexed had Queenie grown at this regular answer that eventually she told Sheila, 'I think your Mam's as daft as a barmcake!' Sheila had agreed most fervently.

The laughter and squeaky chatter of the delighted children filled the air, bringing the women to their doors to smile appreciatively at

Maisie, with her rag-a-bone wagon and her little following army. Queenie muscled her way in, pushing and shoving with such deliberation that the deep barrier of small bodies reluctantly gave way to let her through. Not graciously though, judging by the angry snorts, sly sharp kicks, and loud abuse.

'Give over snotrag! Wait yer turn!'

'Hey! Who do you think you are?'

'Cor! Them bloody boots don't 'arf stink!'

Stink they may have done but Queenie didn't care! Not if that was why they'd all moved aside to let her in, she thought.

Her strong grey eyes widened in amazement as they lit on the appearance of Maisie's wagon!

The spill of bright colour and treasure fair blinded her. The low sides of the wagon were painted in Catherine wheels of gaudy reds, yellows, and blacks; the big wooden-spoked wheels made a body dizzy as the zig-zag lines which wound about them screamed first in gold, then green and ended up in a delightful mingling of black and yellow blobs. The whole wonderful marvellous ensemble was entrancing. The inside of the wagon was filled to bursting and, at the shaft end, where the scabby little donkey tucked noisily into his oversized hay-bag, the piles of old rags and varying artefacts were stacked sky-high.

The remainder of the wagon was loaded down with penny-whistles; bundles of clothes-pegs; goldfish swimming about in little fat plastic bags; big blocks of white stepstone, and small tidy bundles of wood-stick for the fire. Around the rim of the wagon hung more cherry-red yo-yos than Queenie had ever seen in her life. Handmade they were, as Maisie was quick to point out; and polished as shiny as a still pond. They clattered against the clusters of metal-tipped spinning-tops, which also hung in groups of twenty or more from the crowded rim. Then all along the shaft arms dangled hundreds of coloured soft balls, gleaming and winking as the daylight caught the glinting lashing colours within. Finally, every spare inch of space was taken up by the myriads of brightly coloured balloons; so many that Queenie wondered why the donkey, wagon and all, hadn't been clear lifted off the ground to be swept away forever.

'Right then little Queenie! You've shoved your way affront o' these other brats, so what's it to be, eh?' demanded Maisie.

Although Jo's fictional characters are not always based on real people – 'sometimes I put two or three people together to produce a character' – names are often a guide to particular characteristics. If the name

'Molly' is used, we can be fairly certain of the sort of woman to expect. Besides Molly Davidson in *Cradle of Thorns*, who is Jo's mum, there are a number of Mollies in the novels, and in a particular Dedication, Jo refers to a Molly who had known her as an urchin and had watched her grow up and get married. 'Molly was every woman who looked after the children in the street we were in,' she explained. 'She was the epitome of the granny if you like. She'd be in her sixties and she'd be small and round and she'd have a kind face and grey hair and tin curlers . . .'

My personal favourites amongst the old-world characters that Jo fingers in the novels are two fine ladies of mature years, Tilly and Fancy Carruthers. 'They were always in bed,' Jo laughs, as she brings them to mind. 'They would have been deemed lesbians today. They lived right up the top in Montague Street. I knew them because I had a friend who lived next door, Sheila Bullen. Poor Sheila, she married a man called King . . . It was in all the papers – I heard it on the radio – her husband shot her! He shot her while she was holding the baby and the bullet went right through and killed them both. My sister-in-law, Pat, claimed she had gone to see Sheila in her coffin, and she said it broke her heart because the baby was right there, lying at her mother's feet. Sheila was a beautiful girl, long, black, wavy hair, very dark eyes. She was my friend, I went to school with her. We used to run errands for these two old ladies. So many characters . . .'

Here are Aunt Biddy and little Queenie returning the ladies' laundry in a well-plotted trip that takes in a number of characters in the vicinity of their home, before finally arriving at the Misses Carruthers:

The front door was open into the passage. It was always open. Miss Tilly and Fancy Carruthers loved nothing more than to have visitors. They were always welcome, any time of the day or evening. 'Go and tap on the parlour door, Queenie. Tell 'em we've fetched their washing.'

Queenie skipped along the passage, making the very same bet with herself that she had made on every single occasion: that the two old ladies would both be abed and wearing frilly green caps.

Sure enough, on command of the thin piping voice which urged them to 'come in', the same peculiar scene awaited. The tiny parlour reeked of snuff and something suspiciously like George Kenney [Queenie's dad] *when he'd been boozing. The big bed which reached right up to Queenie's shoulders nigh filled the room. The top and bottom of it were like the bars of a jail, and each tall corner was conspicuously marked* by huge shiny brass balls, which distorted Queenie's face whenever she looked into them. It would stretch wide and misshapen, then it would squeeze into itself like a concertina, shaping Queenie's mouth into a long narrow 'O', which quickly vanished into her sucked-in cheeks.

There was real carpet on the floor, and big soft flowery armchairs which could swallow a body whole. Plants reached out from everywhere – from the tiny sideboard, the whatnot, the slipper-box, and even from the shelves on the wall.

'Hello Queenie love. Go and fetch your Auntie Biddy – tell her to push the pram down the passage. It'll save her a few steps carrying the washing.'

Queenie had never seen Miss Tilly out of that bed so she wasn't rightly sure what shape she was, or even if there was any more of her than peeped above the bedclothes. But a good guess, calculated by the tiny pointed face sticking out from beneath the green frilly cap, and the small straight shoulders draped over with a pretty white shawl, told Queenie she was probably right little. Her eyes, though, were huge. Bright blue and stary, with long ginger lashes which looked as though they did not belong to the smiling wizened face.

Sitting next to her, as always, was Fancy Carruthers, nodding and agreeing with everything Miss Tilly said. 'That's right, dear,' she kept saying, 'that's right.' Her features were very grey and wrinkled, and her eyes had sunk away into deep bony caves, which prompted Queenie's silent comparison of her to a skeleton. From the brow of her frilly green cap a strand of thick grey hair hung down the wrinkled forehead. Queenie liked them both. She didn't fully understand their strange goings-on, but she liked them well enough.

It was hard, though, for Queenie to reckon on how it was that the teapot, on the firebrick in the hearth, always contained a hot brew; and the cake-tin on the sideboard was never empty of delicious home-made cakes. They must get out of bed sometimes, she reasoned. But 'twas an odd thing, a very odd thing!

'Climb up here, young 'un. Let's get a closer look at you.' Miss Tilly patted the bolster beside her. 'Yes, climb up, young Queenie.' Fancy Carruthers screwed her face into a peculiar shape of concentration as she seconded Miss Tilly's request.

Queenie looked around at Auntie Biddy, as if to seek her approval. Upon receipt of Auntie Biddy's reassuring smile, she proceeded to hoist herself up on to the cream-coloured eiderdown. It was no easy task, for the bed was high and the soft eiderdown gave way beneath her grasping fingers.

'Come on,' Miss Tilly encouraged.

'Yes, come on,' repeated Fancy Carruthers. Finally, Queenie clasped both her hands round the big brass ball and climbed up along the top. Scrabbling to where Miss Tilly had indicated, she felt as though she'd just climbed a mountain. Sinking into the squashy depths of the bolster, she looked hard into Miss Tilly's eyes, and waited politely.

Miss Tilly grabbed her by the hand, squeezing it affectionately. 'Been helping your Auntie Biddy take the pressing round, 'ave you, lass?' Her features gathered themselves into a tight pointed smile as she looked down at Auntie Biddy . . . 'Fair worn out she looks, bless 'er.'

'Yes,' Fancy Carruthers muttered, her head nodding in fervent agreement, 'fair worn out.'

Alas, nothing is forever, and, given the special nature of a child's first feelings, there is terrible poignancy when, much later in the novel, Jo, as Queenie, confronts and contemplates the loss of Fancy:

Miss Tilly was propped up against a bolster. Her huge watery-blue eyes were now drained of the vivacity which Queenie had always admired so, and their size, which had always been considerable, seemed even more prominent in the shrinking folds of her aged face. It struck Queenie that the smile which had always been perpetual on Miss Tilly's face had developed into a peculiar fixed grimace. A feeling of overpowering helplessness engulfed Queenie as she moved towards the old woman.

Miss Tilly swivelled her enormous eyes upwards to focus squarely on Queenie. 'Hello little 'un,' she piped in an odd shrill voice, lifting a hand for Queenie to grasp, 'Oh, I miss her you know.' She glanced at the pillow beside her, then looked away quickly as though afraid of what she might see. 'Took her away, they did, Queenie, been my darling friend for sixty-odd years . . .' Her wrinkled mouth lifted ever so carefully at the corners and a big pear-shaped tear fell out of one eye. 'Oh, Queenie lass,' she croaked, ''taint the same no more wi'out her.'

When Jo was about six or seven years of age, the Brindles left Derwent Street. It was not a good move. 'The council moved us to a tripe shop in King Street. We didn't use the part of the building that was the shop, fronting the road, but we had all the accommodation behind, and behind that was the river. Before we moved there, in about 1948, Mum used to go in there and buy tripe. In the window there was a big marble slab where they used to put the cows' heels and pigs' trotters. I imagine it was built in the 1880s because it was a grotty place. It became a council house; now it's a flower shop. There was a slaughter-house behind, about forty feet away. The smell was absolutely appalling, and Mum used to say, "Just don't go near there," but we did. It was a place of mystery with strange sounds and it had a dry, sick smell that would come into the house . . .

'The sitting room was about twelve-foot square with a door leading out to the yard,' remembers Jo. 'There was the prettiest fire surround, which had tiles down either side with little pink flowers, a cast-iron mantelpiece and a tiled hearth with a curved fender. In the winter, when the fire was going, we would all sit around and listen to the wireless. There was a peg rug in front of the fire that my granny had made as a present when we moved into the house.

'To the right of the fireplace were the stairs. They were tiny, narrow steps which were so steep we went up on all fours . . . At the top was a little landing and a door to the right and a door to the left. My sisters and I slept in the room on the right with the young boys, Harry and Billy. In our room, another door led to a tiny room where the other boys slept. Mum and Dad had the room to the left.

'There were no carpets – just a bed and a chair to put the candle on in my room. There was electricity, but sometimes the meter hadn't been fed. The only book I had was one I found in a rubbish tip – a leather-bound book of Wordsworth that I cherished.

'It wasn't a happy memory there. Nothing went right. I rescued a red setter there from the dog pound, paid two shillings for him I remember. I worked selling jam jars for those two shillings, and Bernard accidentally let him out onto the road. He went straight under a lorry. No, it wasn't a happy house that one!

'The house had a cellar, quite a deep cellar, which was full of water because the river flooded, and whoever had been in the house before us had chopped half the steps away. You couldn't see that it had half the steps chopped away because the water was so high, but after four steps there were no more, just a huge drop!'

There was indeed a particularly bad spate of flooding in the town in 1946, and the Blakewater, which flows close to the south side of King Street, burst its banks. Houses in the Whalley Banks area, close to where Jo lived, could only be reached by boat.

Jo remembers it was bad, but not unusual: 'Almost all of the houses that we lived in had cellars, though not Derwent Street, and they were often flooded. King Street had a cellar, the next house in Whalley Bank had a cellar, and then the next, Henry Street, had a huge cellar. We kept the coal there of course, and if Blakewater broke its banks and flooded it, then one of my brothers would have to go swimming for the coal down there, bringing up pieces of coal while another brother would wait on the steps with a bucket until it was full!'

Fine cotton yarn is less likely to break in damp conditions, and a century earlier weavers' cottages were deliberately sited close to water and, later, given deep, damp cellars. This is why cellars played so prominent a part in Jo's early life, spent in old weavers' cottages. During a government inspection in 1840, Joseph Kennedy reported finding men and women spinning and weaving in 'cold, dark, damp cellars without any fire or means of ventilation . . . the atmosphere on entering was literally foetid with the breath of the inmates.'

There's a whole below-ground culture in Blackburn, for cellars also played a role in policing the town in the nineteenth century. There was a resident police force in King Street from 1841, but in the days before Blackburn had its own police station, the cellars of public houses were used as short-stay holding places for miscreants – as keeps and dungeons. There is a specific point of interest in the cellars of two pubs, for still today there is a tunnel leading from the cellar of the Duke of York to the King's Head in King Street and thence to the courtyard of the old Magistrate's Court, an impressive building at the bottom of Montague Street.

After the tripe shop, the Brindles moved to Whalley Bank, which, like their other houses, was council-owned. 'Whalley Bank came up while we were waiting for Henry Street to become available,' Jo explained. 'It was a very fleeting visit and I don't remember a lot about that.'

Henry Street, like Derwent Street, no longer exists. It ran between Union and Regent streets. There is a faithful description of the house in *Angels Cry Sometimes*. Its walls were so thin that 'of a quiet evening, if a body walked by, they could almost hear the heartbeat of the inhabitants.' The corridor in off the street was 'a long narrow tunnel of gloomy darkness'. Two doors at the far end of the passage led 'to the "best parlour", which was usually reserved for visitors and in the Bendalls' case remained empty and unused'. The second door led to a sitting room, hopelessly furnished with cast-offs and pieces retrieved from tips, and there was a tiny cold scullery beyond. Then, 'a steep run of stone steps led to the yard below; and in turn to the cellar and the only lavatory ... It was a gloomy, depressing place, devoid of luxury or comfort in any degree. The walls were bare of ornament or picture, and, here and there, large, spreading patches of creeping damp wound their tenacious fingers in patterns of black and green fungus. The only daylight squeezed itself in through a tiny window, which looked out over the backyard.'

However, Henry Street was slap bang in the centre of things, close to the market square, and the sights and sounds of market day come to us from Queenie in *Her Father's Sins* as spellbound childhood reminiscence:

And oh, what a treat it was when she and Auntie Biddy took the walk into town on a market day! Happen they'd be carrying a pair of Auntie Biddy's boots which needed the holes mending. Old Dubber Butterfield would sit on his three-legged stool amidst the hundreds of boots, shoes and clogs which hung from walls and ceilings, then with the great iron hobbling-foot between his knees and with a practised flick of his wrist he'd fit the boots onto it, shape a fresh-smelling piece of leather over the holes and, taking the little nails one at a time from between his teeth, he'd tap-tap and shape until the worn holey leather on Auntie Biddy's boots became a brand new sole.

Just occasionally, the two of them would go into Nan Draper's where every wall was piled high with shelves upon shelves of different sorts of cloth. Brown tweed; herringbone; flannel; winceyette, worsted . . . oh, there was no end to it. And here, Auntie Biddy would purchase her darning wool and thimbles, together with various sized needles. Queenie could remember the purchase of a measure of heavy brown cotton-material only once. Auntie Biddy explained that this rare luxury was necessary in the name of decency, as she was obliged to keep the two of them from 'falling into rags'. As far as Queenie was concerned, she was right glad Auntie Biddy had prevented such a thing. The idea of 'falling into rags' sounded a frightening prospect.

A dilly-dallying walk round the market, though, was something of a magic time for Queenie. Now and then they would stop at the liquorice stall and buy a threepenny bag of liquorice sticks and coltsfoot rock; then perhaps another time they might linger at Jud's corner stall, where amidst the colour and the shouting, the smells of roasting chestnuts and baking tatties, they would enjoy a glass of Jud's black frothy sarsaparilla. It all fascinated Queenie. And she had come to love Blackburn as fervently as did her Auntie Biddy . . .

Queenie loved it all. She derived the greatest satisfaction and enjoyment from watching and listening to all the familiar sounds which carried her above the mundane loneliness and boredom of her own existence. Queenie had always seen Blackburn market as a magic carpet and when a body climbed aboard it would be transported to another world . . . a fairytale

world where round every corner a new adven-
ture waited. So many times Auntie Biddy had
brought her here, and even now, after all this
time, the magic was not lost to Queenie. Tossed
into the hub of activity and camouflaged be-
neath the great umbrellas of red and white awn-
ings which covered every stall down every
avenue, touching each other until the sky itself
was obliterated by this spreading, billowing
roof, Queenie took delight in all about her and
the cautious step of her feet against the jutting
cobbles became a carefree skip.

It is not surprising that there is a central place for
the market in Jo's imaginative vision of Blackburn.
Long before the cotton industry took hold, it was the
fulcrum of life in the town. As early as the sixteenth
century, Blackburn had been a flourishing market
town; five cattle and horse fairs were held annually,
the oldest dating from 1583. And now it was Jo's
own playground.

The market opened on this particular site on
28 January 1848, prompting a local printer and
bookseller, Charles Tiplady, to write verses to this
'day of honour to the Town . . .' The 350-stall bazaar
twice a week – on Wednesdays and Saturdays. It also
hosted an annual Easter Fair, and a year-round series
of speakers, preachers and entertainers.

In *Alley Urchin*, Emma Grady's daughter, Molly,

is taken for a thief in the market. In *Tomorrow the World*, Joe Tidy has a draper's stall there, and in *Cradle of Thorns*, cheeky, one-eared, Irish rag-and-bone-man Joe has a weekend stall, where he sells 'everything from old boots to copper boilers'. In *Whistledown Woman*, Rona Leum, the gypsy, works there while living out at Shillington in the district of Church, and in *The Devil You Know*, set in 1956, Sonny Fareham is fascinated by it: 'All around her vendors shouted their wares, winking and joking as she walked by. Stray dogs dodged around her ankles to snatch up any juicy titbit that fell to the ground, and irate children bawled and screamed while their mothers raised eyes to heaven and wondered why they ever came out that morning.'

The picture is characteristic of many that Jo impresses on our imaginations, poignant and with the tainted atmosphere of a photograph by Brassaï, informed by the particular impoverished circumstances of her youth.

CHAPTER TWO

The Hungry Poor

'Henry Street came into play when I was eight, nine,' says Jo. Despite her depressing description of it, and the fact that here would be enacted the rows that would lead to the family splitting up, she remembers it 'as a happy house – we had lots of laughs in that house'. Nevertheless, 'the hardship was always there and we often went hungry. My mother had an awful job finding the money to feed us, and Sunday was the only good meal we had. We only all sat down around the table on a Sunday. There weren't enough chairs, but everything was dragged out to sit around the table then. She would give us a big enamel bowl and we'd go on the market and collect all the bruised fruit and vegetables. When the market was about to close, all the vegetables would be lying on the ground, so we'd pick them up and take them home. Mum would strip off the outer leaves, wash them all with salt, rinse them, and that would be our dinner. She would cook the vegetables with lumps of meat she got from the butcher in this big bowl and then put it on the table, in the centre, and we would all sit round. And – I am going to get lynched for saying this – the priest would arrive and eat half our dinner! I hated that. He would come in just as she was putting it on the table and he'd help himself and half of it would be gone. I said to Mam, "Why do you let him eat our dinner?" And she made the sign of the cross and said, "It's the priest." I thought, well, he's a selfish priest. "You shouldn't let him come in!" I said, and my mam'd say, "Oh, you've got to let the priest come in." I think they were a little bit afraid of him. He was a Roman Catholic priest of course. My mum and dad didn't take religion . . . they were not sort of fanatical religious people, and I remember the priest would say to her, "You haven't been to church, have you, Mary?" "I'll be along," she'd say. But she never would go along.

Jo's readers may remember the enamel bowl for the Sunday hot pot making an appearance on the table of Lizzie and Ted Miller's house in *Nobody's Darling*. Here, their daughter Ruby explains to her posh friend Maureen what it really means to be hungry-poor:

> *Being poor frightens me more than anything in the world. Money could buy so much happiness. I know that now. All the time our dad's been out of work, our mam's been hard put to*

80

feed the family. I've seen her push her own food on to the young 'uns' plates when she thought no one was looking, and at night when she's sent us all to bed while she waits downstairs for our dad, I've heard her crying. For years, she's worn the same two skirts and the same tattered old shawl. There's never enough food in the cupboard, and we don't have enough blankets to keep us warm, even on a summer's night. In the winter we have to count the number of cobs we put on the fire, and even when our dad was in work, there were times when he had to walk because he couldn't afford the tram fare. Our mam always puts on a brave face, but I know how she's feeling inside, and I can't stand it.

'I am talking about the kind of poverty that you really can't get to grips with unless you have been through it. During my childhood, we never had any cups in our house, only jam jars or milk bottles to drink out of. We had plates because my grandma gave us plates. She was wonderful. But there was only one cup and that was my dad's cup and woe betide anybody who used that cup.

'As soon as I could afford it, I started buying dinner services. At the last count I had twelve bone-china dinner services. They are up in the loft. I don't know why I buy them. Somewhere in the back of my mind I am frightened I am not going to have a cup to drink out of. Now, when I can have whatever I want materially, I haven't changed inside . . . because you cannot forget. You cannot lose it, even though I know that I'll never have to go to the rag-and-bone man again.

'If there wasn't much money coming in at the end of the week, we'd go hungry. But I thought that was how life was. Only when I went to school did I realise we were really poor, that I was different from other people living in better streets. They used to call me Spindly Brindley because I was very thin and had these big blue eyes and white hair.

'We had a lot of well-to-do kids coming to the school from better areas, who were quite nicely dressed, would wear the uniform. I was going to the new school and had to have a uniform. Well me mam couldn't afford a uniform, so she took me down to the rag-and-bone shop. I had to have a blue mac with the belt and hood. Now if you had a penny you had to rummage on the ground to see what you could find, but if you had threepence you could go on the rack – things hanging on coat-hangers! Posh things. And me mam found me a gabardine mac. So I wore it very proudly to school on Monday morning, and we were all lining up to go into the classrooms, and these girls behind me were sniggering and laughing. And I thought, they're laughing at me! Why are they laughing at me? I was ready to fight.

Blackburn was a cotton mill town. The story of the revolution that brought the spinners and weavers from the nearby countryside into the town is the story of how a time-honoured tradition (of both skills and beliefs) was exploited and transformed.

Old weavers cottages in Henry Street, Blackburn, to which Jo moved as a young girl.

In 1830 the male factory operative earned only as much as an unskilled builder's labourer, and it had been better to poor in the country, where you could at least grow your own food and enjoy less obnoxious living and working conditions.

The working day averaged thirteen hours, with forty minutes break for lunch. Much of the work could be done by women, who, it was accepted, could be paid less than men.

'The onset of poverty, real degrading poverty, had crept up on them, in the guise of false hopes. Now optimism was a luxury; yet Queenie could not be daunted.' *Her Father's Sins*

'Caleb Crowther's searching eyes were drawn to the kerbside. There was something disturbingly familiar about the thin, dark-haired ragamuffin...'
Vagabonds

1862, and starvation threatened even the street urchins' games. 'They'd swapped hoops and marbles and traded daydreams, they'd laughed and fought together.' *Jessica's Girl*

'It had often struck Marcia that desperate need, for all its horrors, had a strange way of binding folks together ... There had emerged a kinship between the folk here-about that was strong and comforting.' *Angels Cry Sometimes*

As mechanisation increased the speed and efficiency of the industry, children could take a greater part in the process. Moreover, in the cost-conscious factory system, child workers were popular because they were cheap and available.

'Hordes of cotton mill workers huddled together... their flat caps like a sea of twill and their snap-cans clinking in rhythm with the stamp of their iron-rimmed clogs on the pavements. The streets were alive with the sounds...' *Jessica's Girl*

Mill women in the 1930s, '"Come on Marcia! You shoulda done your dreaming while you were still abed! Or wouldn't the old fella let you, eh?" Marcia turned at the coarse laughter which cut through her private thoughts.' *Angels Cry Sometimes*

The Navigation pub on the canal was Jo's dad's haunt after the family split up in the 1950s. It is also George Kenney's local in *Her Father's Sins*, and figures in *Outcast*, *Alley Urchin* and *Vagabonds* as a haven for pickpockets and ruffians. 'The Leeds to Liverpool Canal was a main artery from the Liverpool Docks to the various mills... It was the first time Emma had ever been inside a barge. Not for a moment had she expected to see such a cosy and pretty home as this.' *Outcast*

Feniscowles Hall, home of the Feilden family, sometime lords of the Manor of Blackburn. When industrial pollution got too much in the late 19th century, the family de-camped for Feniscowles House in Scarborough, miles away, on the east coast of Yorkshire.

20th-century mill owner and Blackburn MP Harry Hornby was known as 'Mr Harry, the owd 'un, the gam' cock,' and enjoyed the loyalty of his workers akin to that of football fans for the team manager.

I'd give anybody a fight if they laughed at me. And I knew why they were laughing when I got into the cloakroom because there was a name tag sticking out of my coat, and it was one of theirs! So their mam had given it to the rag-and-bone man. They knew where I had got it from. So I threw it away on the way home and got a hiding from me mam!'

Jo's novel *Cradle of Thorns* is all about the noble values engendered by poverty and the idea that we are, all of us, born into our own cradle of suffering. How we deal with our particular 'thorny problem' is all. Being born out of wedlock is the heroine Nell Reece's thorny problem. It is a powerful title, and I asked Jo where it came from.

'When I was thinking about that particular book, several titles came to me. I was looking for the *feeling* of how it was for us at home,' she replied. 'Now, my younger brother, Harry, when he was born, I was about five, and I remember vividly my mother bringing him home from hospital and his cradle was an orange box lined with newspaper in front of the fire. That came to me while I was thinking about that book. All of us, all of us children, never had a warm cradle, a pretty cradle. Mum made Harry's box pretty by lining it with a pillow and putting some material in . . . I chose the thorns, I think, because it is evocative of suffering . . . you are not supposed to suffer when you are a child, you are not *supposed* to be uncomfortable, you are supposed to be cosseted and warm and safe. But at home there was never food in the cupboards. We lived each day as it came and life was very difficult.

'My mother always knew when the rent man would turn up and sometimes we would hide down behind the settee and she would dare us to breathe a word. He would go away, but you always knew he'd be back. Sometimes he would try and catch you out. He'd wait round the corner and see if you came out.'

Property men get a lashing in the novels. John Harvey is the unscrupulous property agent in *Somewhere, Someday* – 'a nasty, sly sort . . . mid-forties, fancies himself with the ladies . . . a tight-fisted bastard an' all.' Kelly Wilson gets the better of him and reclaims the sometime family home. Rent man David Miller in *Don't Cry Alone* is a quite different sort, on the face of it mild-mannered and compassionate, but soon we discover that he is a hopelessly weak man, blindly loyal to his boss, Luther Reynolds, who lives in smart Buncer Lane and who is the worst kind of mean, miserly agent, as Cockney Tyler Blacklock discovers from a Blackburn auctioneer:

Right old Scrooge he is an' all. Thinks nothing of screwing the last farthings outta ordinary hard-working folk whose misfortune it is to reside in one of his run-down properties. But, you see, ordinary folk don't get much choice in where they live. My own mother still inhabits a disgusting damp hovel down Larkhill.

He eyed Tyler with curiosity, recalling the distinct London accent. 'Being as you're not from these parts, you wouldn't be acquainted with the facts regarding Larkhill, now would you, sir? Larkhill being a street of back-to-backs, and one of that old fellow's most infamous holdings.' He paused only to draw breath before going on, 'Burned down it did . . . almost the entire stretch of Larkhill on one side. Burned to the ground by a fire started in Maisie Armstrong's place . . . had a lodger she did. The word given out was that the young widder were a relative. Anyway, the fire took Maisie and two other good souls beside.'

. . . 'Since the fire that devastated Larkhill, that canny old villain has wriggled out of every opportunity to put the street to rights. My own mother lives in fear of her very life, what with fire-ravaged timbers hanging loose in mid-air, and rats running free round the rubble. It's nothing short of a nightmare for them that's left in Larkhill, and that old scoundrel still demands four shillings a week rent. Can you imagine that, eh? Four shillings a week, and most poor working folk have only twenty shilling a week between themselves and the

85

workhouse! But do you think anybody gives a
cuss. No, they don't!'

In *Don't Cry Alone*, little Cissie Armstrong, the market flower-seller, lives with her mother Maisie in one of 'the long stretch of houses on Larkhill', up behind Henry Street – Luther Reynolds's patch. Maisie gets seriously behind with the rent, and then she is consumed in a horrific fire, telling Beth Ward in her dying breath to look after 'the childer'. This dreadful scene was once again inspired by personal experience, a collusion of memories that gives the rent man the role of devil in Maisie's living hell.

'When I was about ten I had a friend who lived two streets away from me,' Jo said. 'I loved her very much. She was my very best friend of all; you know, as a kid you do have a very best friend. Her mother had just had a baby, and she was very excited about this. We came home from school that Friday and we were running because we wanted to see the baby. So we saw the baby, and then I went home and played in the street and did whatever I normally did. My friend was going to look after her mam that weekend, as she had just come out of hospital, so she had said to me that she wouldn't be coming out to play, she would see me on Monday morning. I said I would come and call for her to walk to school, which is what I did every day.

'I spent most of that weekend over at my

Grandma Harrison's in Accrington, coming back late Sunday night on the tram and going straight to bed. Monday morning I went to call for Rita and knocked on the door and her dad came out and he was just sobbing uncontrollably. I said, "I have come for Rita", and he looked at me and said, "She's dead."

'I was young and didn't know what to do – you know, you are riveted to the ground, you don't know what he is talking about. What do you *mean*, she's dead? And I just ran home, started screaming and ran home, and my mam sat me down and told me. "I was hoping you wouldn't find out," she said, but she should have known better. She must have known that I would find out. She told me that Rita had been looking after her mother and the bed had been moved into the front room, and Rita had got a little pinny on. Rita was waiting on her mum and helping with the baby and there was a big fire on because it was winter. It caught Rita's pinny and nobody could put the flames out . . . My best friend was burned to death. That has never left me. So, the fire, I think, springs from that time.'

Unlike Maisie Armstrong, Jo's mum never succumbed to serious debt. 'She was working in between having all the children, so she brought money in, but there was always this fear of debt, that you could be carted off . . . She was always frightened of that. It was all swings and roundabouts. The corner shop let my mam buy things against money coming in on Friday, and if the money didn't come in on Friday she'd pawn my dad's best trousers to pay the shop bill. Everyone in our street was poor. And the real problem was the way a week's wages could disappear in the pub overnight, come Friday.'

There was a stigma attached to this, and even today Jo makes a particular point of saying that her father was no different in this to many others. 'It was the same for many people. It wasn't just my father. Some people would hide it. You'd see a man coming down the street and his wife waiting for him literally with a rolling pin. And there'd be a fight on the street, and she'd shut the door and lock him out. So there was nothing unique about it. It was not peculiar to our family.' Similarly, she allows Amy Tattersall her self-respect in *Looking Back*. 'He's no different from any other man in that way,' says Amy of her drunken husband, Jack.

The binge-drinking culture was a critical element of life and features widely in the novels. 'Before the Navigation, the Sun was my dad's Friday night haunt,' Jo told me. 'It was not far from Henry Street, where we lived. On a Friday night my mam would wait, and it would be six o'clock in the evening and then it would be eight o'clock and she'd say, "Tha' dad's not home, lass. He's down the pub, go 'n' fetch him." I was only about seven,

I suppose. You wouldn't do that now, because you'd be terrified your kid would be snatched, but I'd go down the pub and knock on the door and a big navvy would come out. "Aw, it's Barney's lass," he'd say, "fetch her in." And he'd bring me in and stand me on the counter and I'd sing and dance, and me dad would put his flat cap next to me and they'd all put money into it. I wouldn't let him have the money, though. "That's me mam's money, not yours, Dad!" I'd say.'

The Sun at the top corner of King Street appears in various novels, as indeed does the Swan next door, and they are both still there. Old Sal discusses them in *Alley Urchin*; and in *Looking Back*, Jack Mason, Amy Tattersall's former lover with whom she runs away, tells her that 'Most nights I'm to be found in the Sun public house, top of King Street.' In *Cradle of Thorns*, Molly Davidson dares to go in and ask for 'two pints of yer best', and she is ordered out. In 1890, when this novel is set, respectable women were not welcome in pubs. While researching this book I myself met a sometime landlady of the Sun, Rosie Finn, who told me that there were so many pubs in Blackburn in Barney's day that the saying went that if you drank a thimble of alcohol at the Griffin, no more than a mile away, and doubled it at every pub along the way, you would be drunk by the time you got to the Sun at the top of King Street.

With the Friday night binge-drinking came

violence. The pubs were frequented almost exclusively by men, and:

> . . . *there had been more punch-ups and differences of opinion in that* place [the Sun] *than anywhere else in the whole of Blackburn. But it was a long-time, favourite meeting place. On Saturday it was a haven for all those men who sought refuge from the many trials of a working life. They might be seeking relief from a long, demanding week in the pits some distance from their homes, or the mills on their doorsteps, or their wives and families, or they'd be sneaking a quiet drink away from their clinging sweethearts. Whatever the reason, they flocked there by the dozen, propping up the bar and staggering home when the last shout was called.*

By the time of *Looking Back*, a novel set in 1948, young Sandra Craig is not only brazen enough to claim the right to drink in a pub, she openly exercises and abuses that right. But in *Her Father's Sins*, set around the same time, Jo can still write, 'No respectable lass would ever be seen in a pub; unless rightly invited. And even then, they would know their place. So the women often preferred to stay at home and darn their men's socks, bathe their countless offspring and count the dwindling brass which they skilfully hid from the "old man" with his appetite for boozing.'

It was a transition time in all sorts of ways for women. 'A lot of the women were rebelling at the straitjacket that they'd be placed in, particularly in the 1950s. They were going out and they were forcing their way into the pubs. If the men can go in, I can go in, you know?'

We will see that the macho drinking-man culture was bound up with the frustration of a life lived in the ash-pit of an industrial revolution long spent, but that was no compensation to the women waiting in trepidation for their men to come home. No woman today would credit the level of subservience required of the fairer sex in the 1940s and early '50s. 'Getting dad's tea ready was the thing,' Jo remembers. 'He was the man of the house. You didn't have anything to eat until he had had what he wanted. If you had anything it would go to the man of the house. Mind you, there wasn't anything much to eat except on a Sunday.'

The archetypal 'man of the house' in *Angels Cry Sometimes* is, of course, Barty Bendall, Marcia's husband, Marcia being the loosely disguised fictional persona of Jo's mum, Mary Jane. Barty 'drank hard, swore hard, and relentlessly spouted discipline and damnation; ruling his often-servile family with a rod of cast-iron':

The instant Barty Bendall entered the room the atmosphere was charged with fear. An involuntary shiver rippled through Marcia's slim figure, and her expressive dark eyes lost their sparkle. In spite of the forced enthusiasm, her voice was devoid of feeling, perceived only by the ever-watchful Polly. 'Hello Barty. Tea won't be long now,' she told her husband. Looking sharply at Marcia, his whole manner bristling, Barty Bendall grunted acknowledgement.

Wifely compliance meant not only washing and darning and making the man's tea, but waiting up to 'reward' him with his marital rights.

Marcia leaned up on one elbow, fearing, yet half-expecting the worst. 'Drunk!' she whispered into the darkness. 'Blind plaited drunk again, he is!' A rush of nausea swamped her as he continued to shout her name. This was the time she dreaded most – when he came home the worse for drink and demanded the rights of a husband . . .

There was an almighty crash as something hit the wall in the front room. Barty had fallen against the sideboard, his flailing arms sending the ornaments hurtling to the floor, after which abuse filled the air and Marcia prepared herself for what was coming.

92

She waited, the thoughts in her mind a whirl-pool of disgust and indignation. Her lovely eyes grew morose and dim, as she whispered low, 'A pig. I married a drunken PIG!'

. . . Shivering, she slithered back into bed where she lay waiting resignedly for the beast now blundering up the stairs, the tears trick-ling slowly down her lovely face. Her heart thumped with fear: fear of her husband Barty Bendall, and anger at herself for having failed; failed her children, failed at marriage; and most of all, for failing all the happy enthusiastic dreams of her youth.

In the timespan of marriage and the production of umpteen children, Barty changed from being a cheeky fun-loving suitor to Marcia into this drunken blunderer: somewhere along the line she and he had started to bring out the worst in each other. To top it all, a wife would have to undergo these indignities knowing that her drunken husband had squandered the week's money.

'They all worked hard and they all drank hard on a Friday night,' says Jo. 'Because they worked hard, they felt they had the right to drink the money away when they earned it. They all liked a drink; it was a fact of life which everybody accepted . . . except me. Because, you know, sometimes Dad came home a pint or two over the top and would get a bit rough with my mum. I would jump on his back and scream at him and he would just swat me off like a fly. If he hit her I used to run down to the constabulary and fetch a policeman.' As Jo related recently to the BBC: 'I was no bigger than a whippet and I could hardly see over the counter at the constabulary, but he would say, "Oh, has he started again, lass?" And we would go home and he'd tell my dad off. And everything would be fine.

'Then he would be mortified on a Sunday morning that Mam didn't have enough money for food. I was only little, but I would tell him, "You've spent all the money for food!"'

What then? What did these women do when there was no money for food? For Jo's mum 'the answer was the convent, Nazareth House,' Jo recalls. 'The old house, the Victorian house, has gone, but the convent is still where it always was, off Preston New Road. The first time I heard about Nazareth House, I suppose I was about eight, and my mother said one day, "Get your coat on, lass," and she told Winnie to get her coat on and she put the two babbies in the pram, and we walked and it seemed like never ending. I was actually crying I was so tired, and we walked right through Blackburn, right along the Preston New Road, and it must have been five or six miles, I suppose.

'When we got there, she pushed us up this path of beautiful rhododendrons to the house at the top, the big convent, sat us on the benches out front with the tramps and told us, "Sit there." And so we would, and she would knock on the door and the Mother Superior and one of the sisters would come out and say, "It's all right, sit there," and she'd give my mam half a crown and we could run out on the lawn. It was lovely, we'd never seen a lawn! You could actually play on grass! Then she'd come out with a tray of big chipped enamel mugs of tea and great big thick butties plastered with dripping. They'd feed us and give me mam a few bob.'

In *Her Father's Sins*, Jo describes the moment that Queenie arrives at the convent for the first time:

Almost at once they rounded a crook in the lane, and directly before them was a wide open gateway bearing a board which read:

The Convent of Nazareth House

To the left of the broad gravelled driveway, a narrow footpath followed the winding bends up the bank to the convent. Queenie trailed behind Auntie Biddy, her excited chatter temporarily silenced by the awesome solitude and magnificent sights all around her. The whispering willows touched and teased them as they passed by, and the bright songs of birds filled the air with happiness. Queenie felt as though this day she'd been whisked off to paradise.

On reaching the top of the winding footpath, Queenie and Auntie Biddy found themselves entering a kind of open courtyard, surrounded by sweeping lawns and colourful shrubberies.

'Oh, Auntie Biddy!' Queenie could hardly believe her eyes. 'It's beautiful!'

'Aye lass,' Auntie Biddy was slow in recovering from the steep climb and her words were strangled, 'it is that. But I still wonder how folks living in such luxury can ever understand folks like us. It don't sit right in my mind!'

Nazareth House stood proudly before them: a great sprawling mansion of grotesque proportions. Its Victorian origin was evident in the additions of ugly haphazard extensions, jutting out at most peculiar angles from both wings of the house. At either side of the central oaken door, wooden-slatted benches rested beneath towering golden conifers.

Queenie's eyes were drawn to the eccentric-looking figure seated on the right-hand bench. The tramp looked up to meet her gaze. 'Morning, young missie,' he said. He was dressed in a long, heavy black coat which reached right down to the floor, all but covering his thick mud-spattered boots. Around his waist, from the frayed string which secured his buttonless coat, hung various artefacts including a white

enamel mug covered in dark chipped patches,
and a collection of eating tools tied round the
ends by a thinner piece of string.

A few years ago, a television company made a short
documentary film of Jo's life in Blackburn, and
naturally wanted to include a trip to Nazareth
House. 'They had to drag me up there, it was very
emotional for me. This convent plays a very large
part in my memory. Going up through those gates
and coming up through the lane . . . it was so nostal-
gic. Mam had to be a bit desperate before she would
go up there. The nuns used to come out and talk to
you, with their black gowns and white cowl on the
forehead . . . They were very formidable and quite
daunting, but they were kind and they would talk.
They seemed very surreal to me at first.

'I put Nazareth House into Cherry Tree [a smart
area to the southwest of the town centre] when I
wrote *Her Father's Sins*, though the convent is actually along the Preston New Road. I rang up the
Mother Superior to see if I could use the convent for
many of the scenes concerning my mother and she
was delighted, but, "Don't say where we are!" So I
then got all these letters telling me that I had put
Nazareth House in the wrong place!'

Like Queenie in the novel, Jo was her 'own
lass' from a very early age, sensitive to the needs
of her brothers and sisters. 'When we were put in

the council home, when Mam had to go to hospital to have a baby and there was no one to look after us, I was always the one – even though I was fourth in line – who would plead with the matron, "Please don't separate us," and I'd cry and get all upset. The first time we went they separated us – boys were not allowed to be in the same house as girls. So the next time I kicked up such a fuss that they actually made an area in the girls' house where my brothers could come and I could look after them. I was always the one that took charge.'

In Jo's recent novel, *Bad Boy Jack*, we get a taste of what the children felt like being left with the Authorities, when Robert Sullivan takes his two, Jack and Nancy, to the Town Hall one Friday morning. Nancy is barely three, but Jack begins to realise something wrong is going on, although his sense of the father's betrayal is nothing compared to the reader's, who is aware that Robert has every intention of leaving them there for good. Jack, however, is a truly effective character who gives us something of his author-creator as a little girl in just this situation: 'One thing shines through, his devotion to his little sister.'

Another local sanctuary for the poor was the Blackburn Ragged School in Bent Street, close to Derwent Street, and still there today. Ragged schools were originally free elementary schools for poor children. In 1843, Charles Dickens went to visit one in

Little Saffron Hill, London, the very street where Fagin had his notorious den. He wrote that 'the name [Ragged Schools] implies the purpose. They who are too ragged, wretched, filthy and forlorn to enter any other place: who could gain admission into no charity-school, and who would be driven from any church door: are invited to come in here, and find some people not depraved, willing to teach them something, and show them some sympathy, and stretch a hand out, which is not the hand of Law, for their correction . . .'

When Jo attended the Blackburn Ragged School there appears to have been no academic curriculum of any kind, indeed that was not its point. It was more of a Church-sponsored charity. 'If you went there and sang hymns on a Sunday, then you'd get fed. We went there often. From the age of four until I was about nine.'

This is interesting because the academic education of mill workers was not a priority of mill owners in nineteenth-century Blackburn, while they did believe that *moral* education had clear advantages, notably encouraging loyalty to the mill. As a consequence, they were a major sponsor of Sunday schools. 'Those workmen and work women who are most sober, steady, respectable and intelligent have been or still are connected with Sunday schools,' wrote mill owner John Baynes, who had Cicely Bridge Mill and spoke for many with an eye to profitably smooth management/worker relations. Another driving force behind these schools was a determination on the part of the mill master that his workers' families would attend a school sponsored by the church to which he was affiliated. It was all part of a clubby culture with which he controlled his workers.

I asked Jo whether there was a very strict regime at the Ragged School. 'We were never allowed to address any of the women there by their first names,' she remembers. 'There was a woman there, was she called Mrs Parker? I called her Sarah in *Her Father's Sins*. She was very kind. They were all very kind. All volunteers. Christian people.'

'Why did you go there?' I asked.

'All the ragged kids went there,' she replied.

'Why? To have a good time?'

'You must be joking! We had to go into the Assembly Hall and pray. We all had to stand there with our heads bowed and pray. Then we'd get fed. Then, if we were lucky, we would go in a charabanc to Blackpool, and at Christmas time they'd have two queues going down to these big tea boxes, filled with toys that the well-off kids had brought in. The girls would queue one side and the boys the other, because of course there'd be girl toys and boy toys. I remember one particular Christmas, I picked this one-legged teddy, and I had that teddy for years afterwards. I loved it to bits. I mean, we were lucky if we got an apple for Christmas at home, you know?'

I thought of Queenie getting 'a spherical object carefully wrapped up by Auntie Biddy' as a birthday treat, and how grateful she had been:

It was an orange, a big Jaffa with thick pocked skin which shot out gas and juice as Queenie greedily tore it away from the segments. She had delighted in sucking into those fat segments when the bitter sweet juices flowed into her mouth, making her nose sting and twisting her features into such protesting grimaces that might have frightened the devil himself! Queenie had thoroughly enjoyed her birthday treat and she was quick to tell Auntie Biddy so . . .

'Did you not feel that going to the Ragged School was marking you out as different?' I asked.

'I never felt victimised by life, because I love life,' Jo replied.

In 2001 I accompanied Jo to a talk she gave in the Assembly Hall of the Ragged School, as we toured Blackburn together to promote the hardcover edition of this book. She was visibly touched by this her first visit to the school since she was a child. 'When I went into that room, my God, my heart turned somersaults,' she said later. 'I was just that little child again, scruffy and hungry, coming to be fed and watered.'

Queenie turned the words over and over in her mind. 'Blackburn Ragged School'. They had a sad ring about them, and their implications frightened her. She refused to dwell on the matter, thankful that her hand stayed well and truly fast inside the security of Auntie Biddy's.

She looked up now at the mention of her name. 'Queenie! Pay attention, lass.' Auntie Biddy shook her gently by the hand. 'Father Riley's after telling you about your birthday surprise.'

Father Riley led Queenie and her Auntie Biddy over to the long wooden tables, where he gestured for them to take a seat on the accompanying bench. 'Now then, little Queenie, do you want a glass of sarsaparilla, or a nice cup of Sarah's tea?'

Sarah beamed at them from her place behind the serving-hatch. Queenie, momentarily fascinated by the odd face-twitching way Sarah had of hoisting her rimless glasses up the considerable length of her nose, said smiling, 'A glass of sarsaparilla, please.'

Father Riley swept away to collect the refreshments. Queenie's observant eyes travelled the length and breadth of the Hall. She didn't think it a very impressive place at all, more like a big tram shelter, she decided. The woodblocked floor was dull and considerably *worn, especially in the immediate vicinity of Sarah's serving-hatch. The high daunting walls were distempered the most nauseating shade of shiny purple, and the few narrow slitted windows way up towards the ceiling were so grubby that even the bright filtered rays of watery spring sunshine lost their natural exuberance on struggling through.*

Queenie thought it too depressing for words. She began to wish they hadn't come . . .

'Here we are then, one extra large glass of sarsaparilla,' Father Riley slid the drink across the table to Queenie, before handing Auntie Biddy a cup and saucer, 'and one of Sarah's specials . . . There's so much noise in here, Biddy! Perhaps we could talk better in Sarah's kitchen?'

Sarah's kitchen was bigger than the whole of Auntie Biddy's house. Great black iron pans of enormous dimensions littered the endless array of shelves and benches. Three huge cooking ranges, blackleaded and polished till you could see your face in them, stretched away down the centre of the room as far as the eye could see. The red quarry-tiled floor shone with loving care and elbow grease.

Queenie felt pleasantly secure in this kitchen, and it heightened the immediate liking she had taken to the homely Salvation Army officer,

Sarah ... By no stretch of the imagination could Sarah be described as pretty. Queenie tried so hard not to stare at the bulbous warts which festooned the plump smiling face but somehow her eyes were constantly drawn back to them.

'Not very pretty lass, are they?' When Sarah smiled, as she did now, her white even teeth shone like pearls, and her whole face lit up. From behind the spectacles, her fair eyes danced cheekily. 'Haven't always resembled a wart-hog,' she laughed, putting the squirming Queenie instantly at ease, 'one o' these days, I might see what can be done about 'em; but they're no bother! I'm not out to win any beauty contests.'

Queenie decided she liked Sarah almost as much as she liked Auntie Biddy.

Father Riley's quiet voice addressed itself to Queenie. 'Auntie Biddy thinks, and so do I, that it would be nice for you to have a few more friends of your own age.' Queenie knew what he meant. She had no friends really, except for Sheila, and that had long been a source of concern to Auntie Biddy although it had never bothered Queenie ... 'Every Easter,' he went on, 'the Ragged School children have a special surprise treat. It isn't very often that we can afford to go to the seaside; but this *year,' he smiled knowingly at Sarah, 'thanks to help from our Salvation Army friends, we're all off to Blackpool – only for the day mind. Now then, Queenie, how would you like to come?'*

Blackpool? The seaside! Queenie had always longed to go to the seaside, but she'd kept the dream simmering deep in her heart. She knew Auntie Biddy couldn't take her, so she'd accepted that it would have to remain a dream probably for a very long time to come. But now! 'The seaside? The real seaside, for a whole day?'

Father Riley took hold of Queenie's small hand. 'Yes, lass. The real seaside, with shells and crabs, and golden sand. It'll be grand, won't it?'

'Blackpool,' Jo remembers. 'We did actually go once – there were about thirty-six of us in this big chara-banc, and we were all chattering and laughing and fighting on the floor, you know, all that. But when we got there, it was the first time I had ever seen the sea. I was absolutely floored by what I saw.

'This vast space of water meeting with the sky. It was just . . . just mind-boggling. I stood on the sand for ages and ages just looking. It was huge, an awesome experience for me. The space and the brightness, because you know at home the streets were very dark, the buildings, the cobbles. You'd have the lamps, and how I loved the street lamps, and the cobbles . . . but you had this closed-in feeling. Blackburn was a smoky and grimy place, with draughty houses and outside toilets. There was a pub on every street corner and a cotton mill every few hundred yards. The day began with sirens from the cotton mills summoning the workers. At the end of the day the sirens sounded again, the gates opened and out poured the weary figures. As a child I believed the whole world to be the same, until one day when I was old enough to take a ride into the outlying countryside. The shock of those wide open spaces had a resounding effect on me. I realised there was another world with trees, cows, streams and blue sky, instead of one tainted with thick grey smoke.

'First, when they said we were going to Blackpool, it meant little. I had heard of Blackpool, but when we got there I was just so amazed. God knows how long I stood there just staring at the space and this water and the brightness of everything. We only went once.'

Jo's trip to Blackpool was the only occasion she can recall leaving the streets of Blackburn as a child, farther than 'the wide-open fields and tree-lined avenues which belonged to that enviable outer part of Blackburn.'

Whatever the joys of the Derwent Street and Henry Street communities, it is as well to remember just how dreary the streets were. Forties' and Fifties' Blackburn meant smoke and dirt, and smuts and grime coming out of the coal fires in the homes, as well as fumes and chemicals from the industries.

> *The predominant impression which Blackburn leaves is that of grimness, unmitigated by any natural pleasantness, for the city is too large for much sense of the surrounding country to penetrate it. Everywhere is a forest of tall black chimneys, against a sky that seems always drab, everywhere cobbled streets, with the unrelieved black of the mill girls' overalls and the clatter of wooden clogs.*
>
> The Pilgrim Trust, 1938

Jo herself talks of the 'closed-in feeling' of the maze of streets where she played, and of 'the houses dark and grim'. William Woodruff wrote in his autobiography, *The Road to Nab End*, that 'the air hung like lead' after he, as a boy, had returned to Blackburn following his first trip to Blackpool. On the way to school the boys and girls of Blackburn would see nothing but bricks and mortar and chimneys and streets, nothing but dreary fronts of houses and factories.

So, how is it that Jo can also write about the beauty of the townscape in *Nobody's Darling*:

Brookhouse Mills made a daunting and magnificent sight. Like a monstrous stone cake, its grime-covered tiles were the chocolate icing and the long cylindrical chimneys were gigantic candles. The out-pouring smoke snaked through the sky, making weird dark patterns against the bright sunlight which in their very ugliness appeared uniquely beautiful.

Again, in *Tomorrow the World*, which describes the Blackburn community of 1850, she writes:

In this area of King Street, where houses lined the street and rows of chimneys pumped dark, foul smoke into the air, there was little room for beauty. But the bridge was surprisingly pretty, gently curving over the canal, with fluted bricks and narrow pavements. Grime from the mill chimneys had darkened the stone, but it didn't matter. The bridge stood proud, and nothing, no smoke, or the ravages of time, or even the drunks who occasionally emptied the contents of their stomachs over it, could destroy its appeal for Bridget.

Like Bridget Mulligan, Jo's vision of Blackburn is an imaginative vision, contoured by the emotions she experiences. To that extent Josephine Cox is creating Blackburn, just as Blackburn created her. She came to a town of soot and grime and dreary, closed-in streets, and left one of 'real flesh-and-blood people', as she writes in her introduction. Jo's perception is influenced by the spirit of the community, by the character of life, but just as she needed to escape it in her youth, so she would need to be free of it for thirty years in order to make her adult vision coherent. For there were ghosts to lay.

As a child, grim poverty would have been enough to drive her to 'create a little world of my own to get into', but beneath the surface there was another problem, about which Jo loathed to be reminded, but which threatened to find echoes in the grim reality of the streets outside.

Recalling for me how she used to sing and dance on the bar of the Sun gave her 'a warm glow', but Jo, above all, is aware of the compounding effect drink had on poverty, of the repercussions within her family as within the families of many of her friends in her neighbourhood. That is the reason why, in *Cradle of Thorns*, Molly takes it upon herself to cast shame on Len Armitage in the Sun for 'laughing an' giggling an' spending the money yer should be taking home to yer family'; the reason why in *Looking Back*, Rosie Craig, conscious of Frank Tattersall's drink problem, says, 'The drink drives out the man and lets the devil in, that's what me mammy used to say.'

Readers of Jo's novels, readers who have met

characters as violent as George Kenney in *Her Father's Sins* and Barty Bendall in *Angels Cry Sometimes*, know well enough how powerfully her imagination goes to work to resolve any problems that coloured her life as a child. 'All the kids in the street were the same, they all had very difficult upbringings,' she says, ringing a chord in the hearts of thousands. It was this aspect of the poverty of life that threatened to give dire emotional significance to the image of Blackburn as a place where 'grimness [is] unmitigated by any natural pleasantness'. It made clear her dream to escape – 'you know, "*When* am I going to have something different? Why can't my family have something better?"'

A strangely exhilarating sensation swept through her as she emerged from the relative darkness of the mill into the grey daylight behind the wide doors. She felt free! This would be the very first time since starting here that she hadn't spent a full weekday harnessed to the relentless demands of her spinning machine. As the gusty breeze blew against her face, Marcia greedily breathed it in. She'd been used to entering the mill in the dark and emerging at the end of the day, still in the dark. Daylight was something she only ever enjoyed on a weekend.
Angels Cry Sometimes

'There was always a need to escape,' remembers Jo. 'I used to go up to Corporation Park, and I don't know if the willow tree I used to sit under is still there, but it was huge and old and I used to hide under it. The truant officer would go up the park looking for kids, but he never found me.

'It was like being *inside* the tree,' Jo continued, 'and I would look out so that I could see everything but no one could see me. I'd watch the world go by. People, animals, and things that were happening; it would all get clocked into my mind. I don't know where I put it all. I was always an outside person because to be inside was to be in a grim place, cold and grim. To be outside was to be free. If you can get out of yourself, out of the environment which you are in, you are escaping, aren't you?'

Corporation Park sounds so municipal, formal and dreary – anything but a place to which a child of the streets would want to escape. Indeed, it was originally a middle-class preserve. In the nineteenth century, as more and more mills were built, the middle classes began to put the increasing grimness of the town at arm's length, migrating to the fringes (Cherry Tree, Pleasington, Wilpshire, Witton) and taking up residence along the Preston New Road. Here, 'even the air seemed to taste fresher and the sky appeared brighter', observes Emma in *Outcast*, as her uncle, Caleb Crowther, accompanies her on the way to her first day at work in the offices at Wharf Mill:

> *As they passed the grander houses of Preston New Road, the ladies emerged in twos and threes. Some were dressed in flouncy crinoline style, while others favoured the newest bustle line; but all were bedecked in extravagant bonnets, and all were unquestionably elegant and resplendent. It amused Emma to see how her Uncle Caleb's countenance suddenly changed at the sight of all this female finery. At once, he was wearing the sickliest of smiles, and doffing his hat in exaggerated gentlemanly gestures – only to scowl and curse, in characteristic fashion, when a four-horse carriage immediately behind began showing signs of impatience at his dawdling.*

From the 1880s, the Preston New Road carried the tramway and made an ever more distinctive boundary between the working-class maze and the middle-class area of Revidge. It offered the ideal vantage point from which to look down on the warren of mill workers' houses in St Paul's Ward, where Jo was born, and the ideal site for a smart new park. Emma Grady was present at the opening of it on 20 November 1857:

What memories! The mayor and other dignitaries dressed up in the regalia of office and thousands of people from all over the borough assembled to see the park opened. After the opening ceremony, they all surged through the arcuated gateways, some of the women wearing clogs and shawls, others dressed in finer fashion and the men sporting an assortment of flat cloth caps and tall black hats.

Outcast

The land – 50 acres – had been sold to the town two years earlier by Joseph Feilden (the family had been part owner of the Manor of Blackburn since 1721 and sole owner since the early years of the nineteenth century). It was originally intended as a middle-class resort. Hundreds of mill workers, laid off during the mass unemployment and famine during the American Civil War (1861–65), when there was an embargo on raw cotton exports, were employed in improving the park, and it was marked out formally with pristine paths, so that the great and good could see and be seen. It contains two natural lakes – the Can and Big Can – originally Blackburn's earliest reservoirs – and, banking steeply to the north, it carried, at one time, two huge artillery guns from the Crimean War (1853–56) at its highest point.

Corporation Park is a sanctuary for so many of Jo's heroines. For example, in *Love Me or Leave Me*,

Eva and Patsy always go by way of the park: 'here they could skirt the lawns and enjoy the early blossoms – rhododendrons and roses were already showing their colours . . .' It was a haven for Eva 'when she felt lonely. When life seemed to be getting her down she would come into the park and stroll about, or sit and watch the world go by, and it never failed to gladden her heart . . .' In *More Than Riches*, for Rosie Selby, whose mother has been killed in a car accident and whose crippled father commits suicide, the park – and specifically the lakeside willow trees, within which Jo had her den – is a special retreat on cold December mornings. For Kelly Wilson in *Somewhere, Someday*, the park is 'so painfully familiar . . . the place where she had known so much joy.'

One has to remember the imperviousness of Blackburn to any *sense* of the countryside. In Kelly's brother Michael's words, 'the only countryside I ever saw were the lawns in Corporation Park.' One should also remember Jo's point in *Nobody's Darling* that 'it was incredible but true that here the air smelled sweet and fresh, when only twenty minutes' walk away the atmosphere was choked and sooty, the smoke from the mills leaving its grime and odour on every house, street and thoroughfare in Blackburn.' But also, more than this, we should be clear why the air seemed so fresh to Jo, what it was that she found so attractive in the park. She got inside the willow tree and looked out, she got away in those moments, when getting away – escaping from the grim side of life – was what she needed.

Once I began to stay in Blackburn and visit the park I caught something of what Jo drew from the place. My first visit was during school term-time, mid-afternoon, well before the school day was over. I was walking along the tree-covered paths that meander upwards to the summit – no one else was in sight – when I became aware that I wasn't alone. At first I didn't see anyone, only heard the odd rustling beside me in the secondary-layer plantings of rhododendrons and other shrubs. Then, far ahead of me, someone emerged from the undergrowth and stepped smartly back in again when he saw me. It became clear that the place was teeming with life, and I felt like the truant officer seeking out errant boys and girls, hiding, as Jo had done, amongst the boulders and shrub-strewn sides of the hill.

Truth was, Queenie was never at school. Even the Truant Officer had grown tired of fetching her from her various hiding places around Blackburn and there weren't many o' them now that he didn't know about.

Much later, I found myself at the summit, where the Crimean guns had stood, and began taking photographs. While I was there a lad of about ten or eleven came up to the concrete terrace and sat, some way away from me, for close on half an hour, just looking out across the tops of the trees, over the town. He didn't have a Walkman or a mobile phone. He wasn't even smoking, he was just gazing at the wonderful view up there, thinking, or perhaps not thinking, clearing his head, cleansing his mind with the kind of un-thinking that sometimes a young life requires. And I realised that this is much more, indeed quite other, than a municipal park: it is, even today, an escape valve for the kids of Blackburn.

In *Outcast*, Emma Grady is left an orphan and cheated out of her inheritance by her guardian, but after taking the walk I took on that first occasion, she (hopefully like the lad that sat alongside me) got things back into perspective:

Emma felt the urge to visit what had always been her favourite place in the park. This was the very highest point, where the gun turrets from the Crimean War were on display. Emma took the route along the main broad walkway, which would lead her there, via the tall glass-domed conservatories which housed all manner of beautiful plants. As she hurried along the rhododendron-lined walkways, where every now and then the long swaying tentacles of the many weeping willows dipped and played in the breeze, a soothing sense of peace and love came into Emma's heart. Now, rather than

116

grieve for her losses, she gave thanks that at least she still had Manny – her very dear friend and confidante. And here she was, young and healthy, with her whole life ahead of her . . .

It was a magnificent and awesome sight to behold. From here, she could see over almost the whole of Blackburn town, with its sea of graceful church spires, and, standing tall beside these, as many mill chimneys – the former sending prayers to heaven, and the latter sending up black rancid smoke . . . Emma saw a curious magic in Blackburn town, and told herself that, in the whole of her life, she would never want to be anywhere else but here.

A little further towards the edge of town, 'as you go along Preston New Road towards Samlesbury,' Jo explains, 'you come to a lane that's in my novel *The Woman Who Left*, as is one of the farms down there. As you are leaving everything behind you, you'll see a big rolling bank coming down towards the road – open fields, they sweep up from the road. We used to play on there as children.' Here can be found Jo's 'wide-open fields and tree-lined avenues which belonged to that enviable outer part of Blackburn', already mentioned.

The novel takes us along 'the narrow cobbled byways and country lanes of Samlesbury . . . a good fifteen-minute drive into Blackburn'. The particular lane that Jo recalls from her youth is the less than enticingly named Scab Lane, but the scene at Maple Farm is indeed splendid, as Louise Hunter tells, grieving for her late father-in-law, Ronnie, who 'loved this land. It was his whole life':

> *It was a beautiful scene, with the valley sweeping away to the river, seeming to merge with the skies when it climbed away up the other side. The recent showers had quenched the parched earth and now the fields spread out before her, like velvet patchwork beneath the blue, sunny skies. There was contentment here in this lovely place . . . It had an uncanny way of quieting the soul.*

'One day,' recalls Jo, 'I stood at the top of the field, looking down and right down as far as you can see, and the wind was whistling up from the roadway. That became Whistledown Valley in my novel *Whistledown Woman*.' Here, the old gypsy woman, Rona, and the foundling, Starlena, contemplate the spot:

> *From this one vantage point could be seen for miles and miles the valleys and hamlets across an expanse of Lancashire. From the top of the high hill, the green fields fell away in a gently rolling undulation until some four miles in the*

distance they merged with a small wood. Then they appeared again beyond, and from there they stretched away as far as the eye could see. The whole magnificent panorama was breathtaking, awing the onlooker into a profound silence ... Rona came up to seat herself on the boulder beside the child. The two of them gazed out across the world's expanse and lost themselves in the trembling wonder of it all.

Later, in 2004, Samlesbury would also be the setting of the Ramsdens' farm in *Lovers and Liars*.

Jo and her late husband Ken would like nothing better than to get in the car and point it in the direction of the moors beyond Blackburn – one of the most beautiful examples of wilderness in all England. 'We love it. There is everything we like. I really mean that, we lose ourselves. If I had gone there as a child I would never have returned home again.' Yet years ago, she didn't know that such beauty existed just ten miles out of town.

Jo was talking about the Forest of Bowland, a huge open fell space giving life to myriad becks, just north of Blackburn. If you take the plunge into it and push through to the coast at sunset, you will very likely see one of the most magnificent skies of your experience before the light fades and gives over to night. In *Live the Dream* – 'about three different people who each have a secret, private dream –

I think everybody has a dream and you either achieve it or you don't' – Luke Hammond has a cabin there. Musing about his feelings for down-to-earth Amy Atkinson of Blackburn town, he longs to share its beauty with her, and imagines they are in his cabin, 'nestling in the shadows of the fells. The sky there would be darkest black, not faded by the reflection of any streetlamps, and the stars would be piercingly bright in contrast.'

In truth, Jo was a different girl in her youth, her focus the street not the fells, and with that came an outlook more streetwise than romantic. 'I was a load of trouble!' She points me to Patsy in *Love Me or Leave Me*: '. . . she is actually based on a girl I grew up with. She was trouble, too, exactly the same . . . a lot of fun . . . always getting into mischief.'

I encourage the thought: 'Wickedness can be exciting when you're young. That comes across in the books.'

'Oh, God, yes,' she agrees.

'Bringing yourself up on the street,' I say, 'perhaps you were lucky you didn't go wrong?'

'Yes, though not many of my friends went that way. Thinking back to my friends next door or down the street, the ones I used to play with, not many of them went wrong. When I meet them now, most of them have the same values now as they had then. The values that came out of living there. And you looked after each other, you know?'

I asked Jo how she and her friends on the street had viewed the police.

'I was not afraid of them,' she said. 'They were much more in evidence on the street then, but you knew them as friends. To me they were there to help, though I'll tell you one little story. One night we were playing on the bus station near Henry Street, where they used to park the buses overnight, by Blakewater Brook. We used to play in the buses because obviously you could get into them [they had no motorised passenger doors in those days] and we used to pretend to be driving and conducting and all that. One time, this policeman saw us and he shouted out and everyone ran, all in different directions. But at that time I had long plaits, and this policeman grabbed hold of me by my plaits! Lifted me off the ground he did and swung me round. I'll never forget that! He made me promise never to go up by the buses again, and then he let me go home with a clip o' the ear. When I got home, I told me mam, and she gave me a clip o' the ear! So, you see, they were friends, part of the community.'

Stories like that remind us that whatever happened at home, whatever the grim realities of the street, fun was had. And largely it was safe fun. Believing somewhere deep inside that Blackburn was theirs, Jo and her friends ran like fauns in some magic, mythic, lantern-lit land. They didn't just happen to be there, they were part of the place, as surely as the cobbles that dug deep into the street, and every so often a community event came along to prove it.

'Jazzband Night was a ritual every year,' recalls Jo. 'In Blackburn and across Preston and Darwen, it was a ritual, though we were talking about it in the pub the other day and some of the people who come from further out hadn't heard of it. We'd put our hands up the chimney and cover them in soot and blacken ourselves! Everything had to be covered. You could only see the whites of our eyes. Then you'd get anything that made a noise, the old pans, you'd get a stick and beat the pans. Outside the pub you'd go, and the men would come out drunk. They'd give you more money if they were drunk.'

'Jazzband Night' was always an exciting occasion for the children. Falling between Witches Howling and Bonfire Night, the ritual was charged with excitement. The children would black themselves all over their faces, necks and any other exposed parts, until all that showed was the whites of their eyes. Even their clothes were dark so as to merge into the night. Then, armed with every saucepan, frying pan or dustbin lid they could lay their hands on, they would take off in groups of sixes and sevens to bang their tin spoons or wooden sticks on their makeshift 'drums' with enor-

mous exuberance, frightening the life out of anyone who might have been foolish enough to forget that it was Jazzband Night, and sending innocent cats and dogs scurrying away at top speed, their tails between their legs, howling and screeching to the accompaniment of the clattering music.

The destination of these spooky marauders was usually the local pubs, where they'd be sure of catching the befuddled ducks on their way home. If luck was with them, they'd be thrown half-a-crown or an odd sixpence, or even a half-penny . . . it all added up at the end of the night. The money was gladly contributed by anyone who crossed their path, to pay for keeping evil spirits at bay; although the drunks who came upon them were invariably sozzled with spirits already.

Angels Cry Sometimes

I mention the famously huge annual Blackburn bon-fire. In the 1930s, I had been told, it was held in the large backyard of the Dog Inn in Revidge, but Jo remembers it on an open area down in the centre of town by Blakewater Bridge (before the Blakewater was culverted in the 1960s) – 'really where the covered shopping area is today.' It is also featured in *Angels Cry Sometimes*:

When Blackburn Town Hall officials put on the celebrations for the annual bonfire, they really meant business. It seemed to Marcia that every nook and cranny was bursting at the seams. There were more people here than she could ever remember before, and more vendors of all descriptions were peddling their wares, or calling out for eager members of the milling crowd to 'Come and have a go!' There were shooting-ranges; catch-a-goldfish stall, candy-floss and toffee-apple kiosks; roll-a-penny chutes, and many more . . .

Right in the very centre stood the bonfire. No ordinary bonfire this! It was all of twenty feet high and more, with a base circumference which would easily have swallowed the down-stairs area of Grandma Fletcher's little terraced house. If you stretched your neck up into the night, to look beyond the mountain of timber, rags, paper, furniture and anything else that would produce a crackling flame, you would be rewarded by the awesome sight of Guy Fawkes. A monstrous creature, seated in a great wooden armchair, he claimed pride of place right on the very highest plateau. From there, he could survey the gathering admirers below . . .

That very evening the big bonfire would be lit and, following the tradition which had

124

evolved over many years, it would draw great numbers of folks hereabouts, from their cosy firesides. It would light up the skies over Lancashire like some gigantic fiery beacon.

The memory of it sparks the true story of the horse-hair sofa that appears in the same novel. 'My mam had this black horsehair settee. You'd sit on it and it would prick your legs, and you'd leap up off it because it was pricking you. She used to say, "Eeh, I'd luv a nice three-piece suite, you know? Two armchairs, one for me and one for yer dad." And then Bernard came in the night before bonfire night and said he'd just seen two seats and a settee on the bonfire. Guy Fawkes was sitting on one of the armchairs on top of the bonfire. So, when mam and dad had gone to bed, we snuck out, all of us, and we took our horsehair settee and changed it for the three-piece suite on the fire. It was the most ghastly three-piece suite you have ever seen – green with yellow flowers! I can see it still. In the morning, we all got down before her and hid behind the settee to see how she would react. She opened the door, and stood there and stared at it for ages. As we popped out from behind the settee she looked at us and said, "Wor the bloody hell did you get that?!" She knew we'd been up to something no good, but she loved it.'

The tiny parlour was filled with ugliness. All the good furniture that had belonged to old Mrs Bendall had either fallen to bits, or had been sold to keep the food cupboards replenished. The heavy brown sideboard that stood against the window, the rocking-chair in which she sat, the big square table and the few stand-chairs around it, were pieces that had been rescued at various times from local bonfires and second-hand shops, where better-off families had discarded them. The black horsehair settee, grotesque in appearance, but clean and functional, had been deftly removed one dark night from the bandaged feet of a bright Guy Fawkes destined, like the furniture, to be reduced to ashes. The Bendall children, unknown to Marcia, had spirited the settee away, cleaned and dusted it, then set it out in the parlour as a surprise treat for their mam, who displayed the gratitude and enthusiasm that the occasion warranted. Marcia minded very much having to accept other people's cast-offs. But no one knew any better than she did that pride was a luxury she could not afford.

I wondered whether Jo, like Queenie, had ever got into trouble with the truancy officer. She admits that she would often play truant. Her dad would go off to work, her mum would go off to Cicely Bridge

Mill and her brothers and sisters would go off to school, while Jo would go off to Corporation Park, especially if it was maths.

Jo attended St Anne's School, on the Accrington Road but within the Blackburn boundary. 'I hated the maths teacher, he was a monster! He had red hair, green eyes and a long ruler – and I'd go home with my knuckles all red from his bashing.' One day when she decided she wasn't going to school she got the fright of her life: 'I snuck back and, as usual, hid downstairs for a while in case me mam was to come back or anything. And I heard this noise upstairs. I was really frightened because there shouldn't have been anyone upstairs. It turned out it was my brother Richard! He was playing truant as well!

'I didn't like school,' stresses Jo. 'In fact, I *hated* it, except for English. Snake-tongue Jackson, the English teacher, was very small, white hair. We called her Snake-tongue because she had this vicious tongue. You could be sitting at the back of the room and she would throw the blackboard rubber and hit you between the eyes, but she was the most wonderful teacher because she encouraged and she created such zest for learning in us.'

Hearing old Snake-tongue reading from Charles Dickens's *Oliver Twist*, a story inspired by the author's own bleak childhood, Jo was mesmerised. 'I thought, "That could be me. Here's this boy, scruffy and ragged like me." Oliver Twist was someone I could relate to.' His going to the work-house brought back memories of Jo and her siblings being sent to the Authorities' home when her mum was pregnant. 'I played truant a lot but never when Miss Jackson was due to read us *Oliver Twist*. She triggered my desire to write,' Jo says.

Miss Jackson seeded the idea in Jo's mind that she could write about her own experience, that 'if you are born in difficult circumstances, something in you drives you on and you want to get out of it and get above it . . . even if the actual magic [of storytelling] was down to my granddad because he would sit me on his knee and tell me all these wonderful stories. It was a combination of Miss Jackson and my grand-dad who brought out something that was dormant in me. Sometimes I would go to my granddad's and he'd sit me on his knee and tell me magical stories, and I'd tell them to my friends, but I'd also make up new adventures.

'I began to make up stories about my grand-dad and his dog, about friends and family. Then, on Fridays after school, I started charging the other kids a penny each to sit on the bomb rubble in the street while I told them stories. If any turned up to listen and didn't have a penny, I'd kick 'em out. All the week I'd be thinking, "What stories shall I tell?"'

Blackburn was not a prime target of the Luftwaffe during World War II. In fact, in 1939, children from Manchester had been evacuated to the town for their safety. There were only three instances of bombs falling – one in Bennington Street, some way south of the town centre, another at Whitekirk, again away from the centre (to the northeast), and the other very centrally, in Ainsworth Street, close to the market square and Henry Street. It fell just before midnight on 31 August 1940. The damage caused by this bomb very probably provided the amphitheatre for Jo's public storytelling.

The pennies Jo earned from it ended up in the gas meter at home or paid for a loaf of bread. Then one day, when she was eleven, there was a competition at school in which everyone had to write a story about someone they knew. 'The whole school had to enter this competition,' Jo recalls. 'I wrote a story about my Granddad Harrison and his dog and I won the prize – a pencil and writing case. I stood on the stage while Miss Jackson told the school: "One day the whole world will read Josephine's stories." And something happened inside me. That is it! I had decided that I wanted to write my stories and that I wanted everyone to read them. When I went up to collect my prize, the feeling I got when I walked past those same girls who had once laughed at me because of my mac, which my mother had bought from the rag-a-bone, was just priceless.'

Years later, Jo got the shock of her life when she was signing copies of her first book, *Her Father's Sins*, in which old Snake-tongue makes a less than flattering appearance. 'I thought when I first was writing that she must be dead. But one day I was signing copies of my first book in a bookshop in Blackburn and I had my head down and I heard this voice, "Hello, Josephine." And, oh my God, it's her! And she hadn't changed a bit! She came to my first signing session and she was not happy! You see, she hadn't known that the kids called her Snake-tongue until I put it in the book! Can you believe that? And I had thought she was dead!' Jo had to take her away, buy her a piece of cake and a cup of tea and pacify her.

Today, under distinct duress and displaying a heavy frown, Queenie had to suffer Miss Jackson, or Snake-tongue as she was better known. Her tight weasel-face and sneck mouth drove the children into themselves, producing mountainous resentment and squashing any desire to learn. Miss Snake-Tongue Jackson hadn't a friend in the world. She was a pain, a moan, a blind mouth that spouted nothing but horrors. Queenie hated her, and when hometime bell clattered she was off to the safe and comfortable company of Auntie Biddy. Today, after having a warm all-over wash in the tin bath before the fire, and gulping down a bowl filled with dumpling stew, Queenie had helped to fold the day's considerable pile of washing.

Auntie Biddy had watched her yawning. 'Sleepy
are you, lass?' she'd asked gently. Queenie told
her with fervent conviction that it was only that
rotten school and Snake-tongue as made her
tired. Even so, she didn't put up too much of
an argument when Auntie Biddy quietly but
firmly ushered her up to bed.

And so life went on. The sounds of Blackburn filled
the air from early dawn to gas-lamp lighting. Some
men commandeered a piece of wasteland for a small
plot of land and a pigeon coop, and for others, after
the pubs, in order of importance, came Blackburn
Rovers, the betting shops, picture-houses and slipper-baths; 'although rather than waste sixpence on
a tub of hot water at the slipper-baths, the man of
the house would much rather spend it "wisely" on a
swig of healthy ale.'

These slipper-baths interested me. Jo had no idea
how the public baths came to be so named. They
were at the bottom of Peter Street, and presumably
disappeared in the 1960s in the drastic Larkhill
redevelopment. The usual bathing ritual at home
was to bring in the tin bath from the nail on the
backyard wall; then, by surrounding it with stand-
chairs covered with towels or sheets, some semblance
of privacy could be gained. But for a girl just reaching her double years, and passing through that self-
conscious period, it was less than satisfactory, which

is why Marcia, in *Angels Cry Sometimes*, suggests that daughter Polly's increasing embarrassment might be diminished in the comparative luxury of the slipper-baths, housed in the centre of town, in the Municipal Buildings.

However, as Polly discovers to her bitter shame, the point about the slipper-baths is, 'You almost always had to share! And you didn't know who you were going to be sharing with!' Jo recalls. 'Children would share with children obviously, but if it was full up and it was sixpence to have a bath they would charge you threepence and you had to share. And, you know, you could be sharing with anybody!' In the novel Polly has to share, and Jo leaves us in no doubt that she herself must surely have experienced the same embarrassment Polly experiences at about the same age.

Chances are that Polly's sister, Florence, and brother, young Barty, who opted instead to go to the Rialto picture house in Penny Street that day, enjoyed themselves rather more. Here, from the 1920s, a Saturday matinee was shown, originally for the payment of two empty 2lb jam jars, which would have left the Brindle family dinner-service bereft, had it still been a tradition in Jo's day.

The same cinema enriches one of Jo's recent novels, *The Beachcomber*, with one of her best comic scenes. Kathy Wilson revels in her fun-filled and totally irresponsible friend, Maggie, who is forever being sacked from jobs and brings Kathy's heavy emotional agenda to ground in just the kind of rootsy hilarity that has her creator, Jo, screaming with laughter.

Maggie is an usherette at the Rialto, and although Jo would hardly have been a regular Rialto-goer, her description is such that you can almost smell the fusty atmosphere and feel the mock-velvet seats. 'Maggie wasn't actually a friend,' Jo told me, 'but she always seemed to pop up wherever you went. She didn't live that far from us, she used to work as an usherette and she'd flash this torch in your face apparently just to aggravate you, to get you wound up, and she was such a character, one of those larger-than-life people you never forget. She'd be showing people in when the film had already started and she'd be singing, and people would say, "Maggie, shut up, shut up!"'

In the following extract the situation is that Maggie has been warned by the manager about her tactics in dealing with the audiences. She has been involved in several fracas, and the Saturday matinee showing of *The Ghost Ship* proves to be the last straw:

For the first half of the new horror film, every-thing went well ... until a particularly creepy moment caused a young girl to scream in terror. That set off everybody else, and somewhere at the front a child started crying. Then an argument broke out; Maggie, with torch at the ready, set off to investigate. When she got there, it wasn't the children causing the trouble. It was a frail old woman and a burly hunk of a man, who by the time she got there were already in the throes of a heated argument. 'She attacked me with her stick!' The big man was leaning threateningly over the woman's seat in front. 'I'm not taking that from nobody, least of all a senile old busybody!'

The words were hardly out of his mouth when the woman upped with her stick and cracked him neatly on the head. All hell broke loose.

To her credit, Maggie did manage to calm them down, while from the adjoining rows there were shouts of 'Shut up!' and 'Sit down!' There was even a call to 'Fetch the manager!'

The scene goes from bad to worse. The old lady insists on Maggie ejecting the man, who had apparently been kicking the back of her chair. The argument becomes three-sided and the woman gives the man another smack with her stick, which he then snatches from her and throws aside, whereupon, 'she calmly reached into her pocket and, taking out a small snuff tin, she opened it up and threw the contents all over him.'

The chaos spreads; a fight breaks out; the film is stopped; and the manager joins the fray, with ticket lady and second usherette bringing up the rear. When, finally, peace is restored, Maggie gets her marching orders. She goes to the manager's office to fetch her wages, while he sees off the other staff, who are corpsing themselves over yet another disaster on Maggie's shift. Alone in the office, Maggie picks up the telephone when it rings. It turns out to be the manager's wife. Immediately, an idea flies into Maggie's mind, a way to get even:

'Oh, Mrs Ellis, I'm glad you called, I was just looking for your number ... Y'see, your husband's not very well. Oh, no, he's not bad enough to send for an ambulance. He seems to think it is something he ate ...'

'Get him a taxi.'

'I've tried, but I can't seem to find one. So, do you think you could come and fetch him?'

The voice at the other end shook with anger. 'I suppose I'll have to ...'

Maggie brings the conversation swiftly to a halt as the manager re-enters the room. He begins to pore over his adding machine and sort out what Maggie is owed. Engrossed in what he is doing, he bags her wages and passes them across the table, only looking

up when she says nothing at all in response, whereupon he gets the shock of his life:

*While he had been tapping away, Maggie had
been undoing her jacket. Now she stood before
him with her breasts in all their naked glory!
'Jesus!' His face went a purple shade of red and
the sweat broke out in torrents down his back.
'Put your clothes on, woman, before somebody
comes in!' His eyeballs swivelled to the door
and then back to Maggie, and with his mouth
open he gaped at her, positively dribbling. 'You
little vixen.' He tried hard to hold the smile
down, but, like a certain other part of his body,
it popped up, out of control. 'Maggie, behave!'
In truth, Maggie behaving was the last thing he
wanted.*

*. . . Sliding up to the desk, she leaned over,
her rather ample breasts almost touching his
face as she purred invitingly, 'I thought we
might say our goodbyes properly . . .'*

*Realising what she meant, he gulped so hard
that his Adam's apple bobbed up, getting stuck
for a minute, before it bobbed down again.
'Oooh, whatever will I do with you?'*

*It was all she could do not to laugh out
loud. 'Whatever takes your fancy,' she said and,
grabbing him by the collar, drew him forward,
planting the longest, wettest kiss of his entire*

life on his open mouth; by which time he was
putty in her hands.
    A few minutes later, with Maggie in his arms,
the door opened and in walked his wife.

Later, Maggie would relive the events for Kathy in a
letter: 'When his wife walked in, I started crying an'
screaming about how he'd taken advantage of me,
poor girl that I am. She offered me money to keep
my mouth shut . . .'

For wannabe teenagers in the 1950s, the nearest
you got to a groove in Blackburn was Teddy's shop,
still there today, on King Street. 'He would sell you
a pennyworth of sarsaparilla. Three of you would
just sit there, and you'd have a penny which you
would go and earn. Sarsaparilla was a forerunner to
Coca Cola.'

Jo featured the tiny place in her first novel:

It was only a ten-minute walk to Teddy's shop,
off the High Street and down a cobbled alley.
Teddy was a twisted dwarfed figure, with huge
pink eyes and a bald head. His little shop, well
known throughout Blackburn, sold the finest
herbs, spices, Woodbines and snuff. It was a
delightfully quaint old shop, with layers of deep
shelves from floor to ceiling. Each shelf was
crammed with jars containing green rosemary,
black liquorice, wood sticks, brown snuff, pink

and yellow barley-twists and hundreds of other colourful herbs and remedies of all shape and description. It was said that he knew how to cure everything from a toe-ache to a broken heart.

The deep glass-fronted counter where you paid your purchases was filled with spacious tubs of different-coloured Khali, a kind of fizzy sherbet powder; along the floor against every wall stood enormous stone bottles of sarsaparilla; a delicious tar-coloured liquid which stung your nose and brought tears to your eyes. A long narrow glass of sarsaparilla was a real treat and was usually drunk in comfort and leisure on the 'staying seat'. The staying seat was tucked away out of sight behind a green curtain. Anyone fancying a measure of sarsaparilla just sat themselves down on it, and waited for Teddy to serve them.

Then, every Easter came the fair – and not just any fair. They held it on the old market square, and it had a long, well-tried pedigree. For instance, in 1849, writes Derek Beattie – the 'main attraction was a large-headed girl, rabbit-eyed children and a lady giant . . . Boxing, ring tossing, popgun shooting, wheels of fortune and sword swallowing made up a few of the sideshows.'

'The Fair! Mam! I can 'ear the fair! I can smell the baked tatties!' Young Barty's feet barely touched the ground, and his little flat cap bobbed about excitedly as he hopped and jumped, ears straining, towards the tinny rhythmic tones wafting towards them on the breeze. In that miraculous way that children have, young Barty had opted to put the distasteful memories of the earlier scene out of his mind; 'Oh go on, Mam! Please,' he insisted, 'please let me 'ave a ride on the 'orses.'

Florence hurried to keep up. 'Yes, and can we all have roasted chestnuts?' she pleaded.

'We'll see,' Marcia laughed . . .

As the family turned the corner on to Ainsworth Street, the whole colourful scene lay before them like the setting on a stage, only this was real!

The music filled Marcia's soul with joy as she perused the busy scene. It seemed as if the whole world and his friend were here to enjoy the festivities. The area was decked from one end to the other with twinkling lights, and from every corner there came the shouts of excited stall-holders clamouring for attention. There was no official entrance as such, but the positioning of stalls and stages dictated points of access, and flanking every path colourful enterprising characters had set up their varied *diversions. At the junction where the stalls split away to either side, a little wizened man had placed his barrel organ in a shrewd position, so that anyone emerging from Ainsworth Street had no choice but to pass him before reaching the centre of activity.*

'Everybody loved the fair,' agreed Jo. 'There was a woman who used to come with it, she had her own caravan and a daughter who was fifteen when my sister was about twelve and I was about ten, and she would give us clothes and shoes and great big earrings and things, and we'd dress up. They were long – it was silly really, they were too grown up for us, but we loved them and we'd go round in them. Things you never want to forget. The fair was magic, magic!'

I asked whether her family could afford to go on the rides. 'We used to *work* on the rides. We used to collect the money. It could be quite dangerous. You know the caterpillar thing that goes up and down? My brothers used to collect the money there. Myself and my sister Winifred used to work on the hoopla, collecting the money.' This must be why Jo lets Polly win on the hoopla in *Angels Cry Sometimes*, knowing how unusual an event winning on the hoopla is: ''Ere, 'ave you done this afore?' demands the woman working on the stall that night, looking for an excuse not to pay out.

140

'We got very friendly with the people who owned the fair and the stalls,' Jo told me. 'They were gypsy characters, tough they were. You'd see many a fight, bare knuckles.' I mention *Looking Back*, the novel in which Alfie, Molly Tattersall's boyfriend, is a bare-knuckle boxer. 'When I saw them fighting behind the fair on the spare ground,' says Jo, 'they would knock hell out of each other. And apparently they used to do this fighting everywhere and I looked into it. Ireland was very well known for it. They would do this not just for play, but for real, really going at each other.'

At the fairground in *Angels Cry Sometimes*, we see Marcia Bendall, queen of all those beleaguered, loving but mistreated, matriarchal figures that are conjured up in the image of Jo's own mother, expressing with rare sensitivity the nature of the burden these women carry; their loss, if you like.

Marcia's husband Barty has died. Little Ada Humble's husband Toby has likewise come to grief (in his case on his Saucy-Sally, the large iron bike he would ride unsteadily back home from the pub when he'd had one too many). So there is emotion in the air, and what follows in the novel is once again sourced in an episode of high emotion etched in the author's memory:

'My most vivid memory of the fair,' explained Jo, 'was this big generator wagon. The front of the wagon dropped down, so it was like a big shop, and they used to sell things from it, but now and again they would have someone singing in there, singing over a Tannoy. That was where me mam sang this one time. She chose "Danny Boy". She used to love singing but she only did it the once in public. I remember all us kids were down there and there had been a man singing and it was absolutely beautiful. But then, on this particular night, my mam got up and sang. I couldn't believe it, I was so proud. Never had she had a chance to express it. We were mesmerised.'

The song became a story, and the story breathed life, and Marcia's voice was never more magnificent. For a few precious moments time rolled back and once again, each heart knew the joy of embracing a loved one. They knew also the despair when one was taken.

There was nary a sound from the four hundred-strong audience. Even the stall-holders and fair-folks had brought their churning machinery to a halt ... Marcia's caressing words bathed the cool night in a soft gentle warmth, weaving a magic spell ... [and] when the song drew to a close, the crowd stood transfixed. Then, of a sudden, the silence was broken. The cheers that had caught in the choking fullness of their throats broke through in

waves of shouts and whistles, all praising
Marcia and all wanting more.
'God bless you, lass.'

CHAPTER THREE

Stratagem and Strife

In order truly to understand how the elements of working-class culture thread the people of this area together – the warp and weft with which Josephine Cox weaves her spell – we must expand our horizons and go back to a time when Derwent Street was an undisturbed, green and pleasant strip of land. For the paradoxes that marked Jo's life in post-war working-class Blackburn, and now preoccupy her as a writer, are the paradoxes of the culture in which she took root. Therein lie the seeds of pain and laughter, the violence and love, the exploitation and pride, the alienation from nature and peculiar sense of belonging it induced.

Peasants living in this area before Blackburn began its nineteenth-century industrial sprawl, had, for hundreds of years, been engaged in the business of weaving cloth. They were part of a tradition – a rural, not an urban, tradition – that went back centuries. It was other than a job, it was a way of life; indeed it was a whole unconscious philosophy of life, a way of surviving in the countryside, free from bondage to an employer. Theirs was a tradition not only in the sense of craft customs and the skills of spinning and weaving (though they were of course part of it), but also in the sense of beliefs and the very character of life. So important was this tradition that when the revolution swept it aside, there arose a requiem to it, an inspired outpouring of Blackburn poets, loom workers and the like, who would recite their works at a spot on Blakeley (now Blakey) Moor in the centre of town.

The story of the Industrial Revolution, which enticed these people to de-camp from the countryside into the town, thereby participating in the biggest social change Britain has ever seen, is the story of how their time-honoured tradition was both exploited and transformed and how a certain dogged moral, even spiritual, dimension of it enabled the weavers and spinners to survive the horrors that lay in store, their struggle setting the stage for a twentieth-century culture of human rights.

The craft way of life was, originally, as close to nature as farming. The natural environment – the local soft water and damp climate – favoured it; it was undertaken in the countryside; and it dovetailed with living off the land. At first, spinning and weaving were a way to eke out incomes from land-based labours, especially during the barren winter months.

The crafts were undertaken at home, the finished material sent from outlying villages by packhorse and wagon into the town to be sold. The cotton and linen yarns were spun on a simple treadle- or hand-powered spinning wheel, and the yarn was woven into cloth on a hand loom. Long hours were spent in the process and it was physical work. Generally, the men of the household would do the weaving, the women the spinning.

Spinning a continuous, twisted strand of natural cotton fibres, each of which is short and about as fine as a human hair, spinning a yarn as we say, is probably as old as the art of story-telling itself – Indian and Egyptian records of the craft take us back to 3000 BC – and the pun is not arbitrary. There has long been an association between looms and literature. I have already mentioned the Blackburn poets, central to whose work is the poetic celebration of the hand-loom weaver tradition, but Blackburn is not the only town to produce weaver poets: in the same century Longfellow found the same in 'Nuremberg', where the 'flowers of poesy bloom . . . in the tissues of the loom.'

What is noticeable is the moral vein that these poets let in the characterisation of the weaving tradition, and it is that vein on which we will see the Industrial Revolution going to work. 'Owd Peter', Henry Yates's portrait of an old hand-loom weaver, is a man honest and proud to his core:

146

Owd Peter wer a gradely mon,
As ever breathed a pray'r;
His record stood abeawt A1,
For wod were reet an' square . . .

He put his picks in straight an' fair,
An' ne'er his duty shirk'd;
No mooter fell to Peter's share
Fro' ony sooart he werk'd
Th' owd putter-eawt could trust him weel,
An' when t'brisk times wer gone,
Peter could use his troddle heel,
An' mek a potterin' on . . .

Joseph Hodgson, born in 1783, was another Black-burn weaver and poet, as was Richard Dugdale, a parish apprentice, born around 1790, who never had a day's schooling in his life and became known as 'the bard of Ribblesdale'. In *Poets & Poetry of Blackburn*, published in 1902, George Hull, himself a poet of the town, puts the very unusual number of men writing and reciting poetry in Blackburn down to the depth of need for imaginative escape from 'the smoke and smudge of the factory and the foundry', and he points to 'those beauties of nature which may be found so plentifully scattered around him, as soon as he has climbed any of the hills that encircle the town itself.'

Certainly these poets are inspired by beauty. There

are poems that extol the natural beauty of the nearby countryside, and there are poems like those of hand-loom-weaver-turned-factory-operative John Baron that bewail the loss of beauty in Blackburn itself, as the revolution gathers pace and the weavers and spinners are drawn by need to the increasingly industrialised town, and looking back to a time in the town itself when it was 'blessed by many a green nook'.

The Industrial Revolution squeezed nature out of the town with Judgement Day finality. As Jo wrote in *Angels Cry Sometimes* of the neighbourhood of her home in Henry Street: 'There were no seasonal changes, each day being a continuation of the day before, and even the birds sought brighter climates.'

But the loss of beauty that these poets mourn is not only in nature. They are looking with sadness to an era that is passing before their very eyes, to a rural tradition in transit, to an idyll that the Industrial Revolution is sweeping away, to the autonomous, rurally-based lifestyle of the independent hand-loomer and to deep-rooted values that will, over the next 150 years, be transformed by the urban factory system, the mill masters' greed and the conditions they impose. They are looking back, in effect, to the innocent 'childhood' of Blackburn's history.

Richard Rawcliffe was born in Ribchester in 1839, where he became a hand-loom weaver before moving the few miles to Blackburn to work on a power loom, eventually becoming an overlooker. First, in Rawcliffe's 'Idylls by the Hearth', comes tradition in sweet, rural process:

> *Another weary day had fled, –*
> *The fire was burning low and red;*
> *'Twas late, my Ruth and babes in bed*
> *Were soundly sleeping.*
>
> *Outside the door the wintry rain,*
> *Came tapping at the window pane;*
> *When calmly, softly, to my brain*
> *Sweet thoughts came creeping.*
>
> *The mouser watched beside the hole;*
> *The cinders one by one did fall,*
> *And darkly on the kitchen wall*
> *Were shadows flitting;*
>
> *And many an old familiar face,*
> *Among the cinders I did trace,*
> *While I, in my accustomed place,*
> *In thought was sitting. . . .*

The hand-loom weaver is in tune and in time with the rural scene around him. There is complete empathy, and from nature herself he draws the deep-truth values that characterise the tradition that he is living, values which, in the following extract, bestow on him the title of working-class hero, an epithet that would endure in spite of the revolution, and be the twentieth-century working-class rallying call:

> *. . . The man who glories in the right:–*
> *In honest toil 'neath virtue's wing:*
> *He struggles hard from morn till night,*
> *And calmly bears affliction's sting*
> *To get the needful things of life,*
> *And nobly thus he battles through*
> *The falls and bruises of the strife:*
> *Methinks that man's a hero too.*
>
> Extract from 'Heroes'

The Blackburn poets were hard working men, and there were lots of them, which is surprising. Would one not have expected hard men such as these to have despised the form as esoteric? Not if one is to believe J. C. Prince, who was one of them:

> *If, 'mid the world's rude shock and strife,*
> *Thou hast no sense of things divine,*
> *No longing for the holier life, –*
> *Oh, what a priceless loss is thine!*

There were tradesmen, too, like Robert Clemesha, a grocer and tea dealer who stored his verses 'among his pepper an' his 'bacco an' his snuff' in his shop on King William Street. Some of these poets were published in book form, others published themselves on broadsheets, selling them wherever they went. John Charlton, a cobbler also living close to the Market Place, railed in his poetry against the exploitation of the working man and spread his works around the local pubs. Liking a drink, he also 'furnished fun and amusement for many a bar-parlour' with his favourite songs, such as 'The Mayor of Mellor', 'Yer Margit's Sister', 'The Poet's Prince', and raised a glass or two with 'The Miser Landlord' and 'The Brewer's Coachman'.

It might have served Jo as a child to have alluded to Charlton when her father dismissed her own literary aspirations. 'When he came home from a hard day's work,' she told me, 'the last thing he wanted to hear was any of my airy-fairy nonsense.' Yet a century earlier it was exactly what the hard-working, hard-drinking Blackburn man *did* want to hear. In a very real sense, Jo belongs to this tradition.

A respect for the truth-divining form of poetry, and in particular for its Romantic propensities, may have been encouraged in Blackburn by a lingering sense of the pantheistic superstitions common in earlier times. For, in the seventeenth century, spinning was not the only craft able to claim continuity with a rural culture thousands of years old.

On 18 March 1612, on the road to Colne, a woman called Alison Device, native of the Forest of Pendle, close to what is the M65 northeastern approach to Blackburn today, begged for some pins from a pedlar and was refused. Device cursed the man, apparently paralysing him. Brought to account, the woman confessed to practising witchcraft, implicating her mother, Elizabeth Southern, and another local, Anne Whittle. As these women were known respectively as Old Mother Demdike and Old Mother Chattox, it might seem a fair bet that they were indeed witches, and sure enough, tales of them turning ale sour at the inn at Higham and using a clay doll to bewitch the landlord's son, causing his death, were soon widespread.

Later it emerged that each of the two women had a following at odds with the other's, the son-in-law of one of them paying the other old woman in meal for his own protection, and the two witches vying with each other to claim responsibility for any atrocities that occurred in the area.

Alison Device was committed for trial at the Lancaster Assizes, along with the two dames and Anne Redfern, Anne Whittle's daughter, all of them held at Lancaster Castle. Within a week of their committal, as Thomas Potts, Clerk of the Assize Court, recorded at the time, 'at Malkin Tower in the Forest of Pendle, upon a good-fryday,' there gathered together 'all the most dangerous and wicked and damnable witches in the country, far and near . . . In their great assemble it was decreed [by the witches] that M. Covell by reason of his office [he was the gaoler at Lancaster Castle] shall be slain before the next Assizes, the Castle of Lancaster to be blown up.' Malkin Tower is believed to have been on Blacko Hill, to the east of the region, and some of those alleged to have participated in this meeting were carted off to Lancaster Castle too.

In total, nineteen people were imprisoned at Lancaster, charged with practising witchcraft. Eight came from a village called Samlesbury, by what is now the A677 northwestern approach to Blackburn, although only three of these so-called Samlesbury witches were actually brought to trial, namely Jennet and Ellen Brierley and Jane Southworth. Their accuser was fourteen-year-old Grace Sowerbutts, Ellen Brierley's granddaughter. The charge was that the women had conspired by 'witchcrafts, enchantments, charms and sorceries', at times in the guise of a black dog, to cause Grace's body to become 'wasted and consumed'. The full text of Grace's testimony is extraordinary, violent and very strange.

In the case against Jane Southworth, however, the court perceived a pretext for the charge against her in the then current political upheaval in the established Church. She was the daughter of Sir Richard Sherburne of Stonyhurst, home today to the well-known Roman Catholic public school, a few miles north of Blackburn. She was also the widow of the grandson of Sir John Southworth, the sixteenth-century Lord of the Manor of Samlesbury, whose strong Catholic beliefs and allegiances had made him a front-line supporter of Mary Queen of Scots. Later, in the reign of Elizabeth I, Sir John, while still Sheriff of the County, had been imprisoned and fined for speaking against the Book of Common Prayer. By the time of the witches' trial, in 1612, Mary's son James I was on the throne, and his vacillations between the Protestant and Catholic camps had served only to exacerbate religious passions. In this context, Jane Southworth, a member of a principal Catholic family, had decided to become a Protestant, and the court concluded that the case against her was part of a family-inspired Catholic strategy to disgrace her. In the end, Grace Sowerbutts did admit that she had been counselled by Christopher Southworth to fabricate the case against all three women.

Nine of the lower-order Pendle witches and their accomplices were hanged, however, and surviving records of the testimony against them leaves a clear impression of a people in touch with the supernatural. Sorcery and spinning are, indeed, the very stuff of scary fairytale, and *Sleeping Beauty*, the story of a fairy uninvited to the christening of a king's daughter, who then spitefully curses the little girl, pronouncing that she will wound herself on a spindle and die (later converted to a sleep of a hundred years), is redolent of this period and was first published in the seventeenth century by the French raconteur, Charles Perrault.

Superstition was a theme of life throughout Britain at this time, but the Pendle Witches affair was highly visible and is interesting also because of the wide social range (from aristocrat to beggar) of the defendants. Soon there would be a different spirit alive in the land, one that would pull up by the roots the lives of many who lived in this ancient rural context. The eighteenth-century Age of Reason swept superstition aside and prepared the people of Lancashire for two centuries of invention, materialism and entrepreneurship, the like of which the world had never seen and could not have imagined.

But their sense of the supernatural was only ever driven underground, as perhaps was the craft of weaving a spell. In *The Road to Nab End*, William Woodruff recalls stories current when he was growing up in Blackburn in the twentieth century of witches on Pendle Hill, elves in the roots of trees and under rocks, a white lady haunting Samlesbury and ghostly horsemen across the moors. A belief in Fate remained especially strong – Jo herself is a strong believer in it to this day, and many of her novels evince this belief, explicitly in *A Time for Us* and *Jessica's Girl*: 'There's no use fighting it . . . These are the cards you've been dealt, Phoebe Mulligan. Play them with the courage your mother gave you. And don't ever shame her.'

Commonly, still, people see omens in things, and in East Lancashire, Halloween attracts so many revellers to Pendle Hill that a police presence is required to keep traffic moving. We should not, therefore, be so surprised to find hard working men with a 'sense of things divine' – the Blackburn weaver poets – capable of charting their own history through the hothouse of the Industrial Revolution into the twentieth century with sensitivity to the spirit of place and people.

As I showed in the *Introduction* the move from country to town came as a result of a gradual modernisation of the cotton industry over 200 years from the early seventeenth century, with eighteenth-century inventors, particularly of the power loom, accelerating the change from rural cottage industry to urban factory process, and with the canal and railway expediting the revolution in the nineteenth century.

In Blackburn, resistance to the hijacking of the traditional domestic industry began early. The first mill to take on a spinning jenny had been Peel's Mill. In 1768 rioters ran amok, attacking both the mill and inventor James Hargreaves's cottage. The mill belonged to the family of Sir Robert Peel, British Prime Minister 1834–35 and 1841–46, founder of the Metropolitan Police and instrumental in the repeal of the restrictive Corn Laws. He was born in Fish Lane, Blackburn, twenty years after the attack, but the family was eventually driven out by worker riots.

The cottage spinners and weavers were not about

to give up their freedom without a fight and their passions were whipped up by the putter-outs, the middle-men who would lose their livelihoods in the new factory system. Worse, the new mill owners instigated a deliberate policy of cleansing the countryside of the old tradition.

A common view in the history books is that enclosures and new agricultural methods were displacing the rural people anyway. But a government enquiry in 1838 reveals a mill-owner strategy of rural depopulation, of coercion and oppression, of herding agricultural workers, hand-spinners and weavers from their cottages in outlying villages into the new mill-worker colonies in Blackburn, of mill owners buying up hand-weavers' cottages, evicting their tenants and then offering them salvation in the form of jobs at their Blackburn mills. It is small wonder that the weavers turned nasty.

In his autobiography, William Woodruff describes the legal backlash – how workers who had burned factories down were transported to Australia and paid with their lives. In 1812 in West Houghton they hanged three men, and a boy of fourteen went to the gallows calling for his mother. In the 1820s in Blackburn, thousands of workers, armed with pikes, hammers and crowbars smashed every power loom they could lay their hands on.

April 1826 saw the last riot. It came just a year after power looms had been installed in Dandy Mill, and at a serious downturn in the industry which saw more than half the population of Blackburn on poor relief.

Six thousand rioters participated. The Bay Horse Hotel, in the Church Street/Salford Bridge area, was occupied and drunk dry, and more than 200 power looms were wrecked. One John Hartley was amongst the rioters arrested by the High Constable's men. His family had been in cotton for 100 years, since Thomas Hartley, 'a poor boy of Blackburn', was apprenticed as a weaver in 1730. Many of those arrested were committed for trial at the Quarter Sessions, though not Hartley himself, whose family would remain in the industry until 1991.

Reading such a statistic underlines the reality of the living continuity of the tradition, and recommends the historical approach in attempting to understand what it was that made the Blackburn community tick at any period, at least up to the mid-twentieth century when Jo was soaking it all in. This is, of course, Jo's own approach; the story settings of her novels range from 1850 (*Tomorrow the World*) to 1985 (*A Time for Us*).

The hand-loomers failed to stop the revolution, but, as Beattie points out, they probably did delay the mechanisation of the industry

What they went through deeply affected and hardened their character, fusing them into a community. Certain values rose up within the community to become its characteristic expression: a survivor-sense of self-worth, a resolution born of never getting something for nothing, a work ethic born of want and driven by what Woodruff describes as 'tight-lipped, dogged pride'. Work became, as Chris Aspen notes in *The Cotton Industry*, 'a virtue to be culti-vated', and less doughty men abroad became wor-ried lest the trait be catching. In 1844, Frenchman Leon Faucher wrote: 'Overwork is a disease which Lancashire has inflicted upon England and which England in turn has inflicted upon Europe.'

All this in the face of often terrible working con-ditions in the mills. Besides the noise of machinery already mentioned, there were some extraordinary environmental problems, such as the pumping of unclean water as steam into the factories in order to create an atmosphere favourable to the production of fine cotton yarn. Not only did this tainted steam produce an unhealthily polluted atmosphere in which to work, but the contrast with the atmosphere outside encouraged further infection and disease.

In 1830, the working day averaged thirteen hours (six a.m. to seven p.m.), with a forty minute break for lunch. This might seem better than the sixteen-hour day frequently worked by the traditional hand-loom weaver, but the factory operative earned only as much as an unskilled builder's labourer. While in times of depression, the rural hand-loom weaver might have failed to earn enough to feed his family, it had been better to be poor in the country, where you could at least grow your own food and enjoy less obnoxious living and working conditions.

The wage problem in the cotton industry had to do with hand-workers being traditionally ill-paid and the fact that much of the work could be done by women, who, it was accepted, could be paid less than men. The new mill owners saw no reason to change this state of affairs. Amongst factory operatives in the early 1900s, females outnumbered males by two to one, and 44% of all married women in the town worked. A cotton-mill family might find consolation in the fact that female as well as male members could find work in the industry, but so poor were the wages that it took two to feed a family, and if, for whatever reason, there came a time when no more than one member of that family was fit or able to work, he or she would not be able to earn enough to make ends meet.

While the machines of industry grew, the machinery to run this new society lagged far behind. We read of 'heaps of refuse, debris and offal', of hopeless drainage, of standing pools and a terrible stench.

In June 1849, Charles Tiplady wrote a letter bewailing the pollution that industry had brought to the Blakewater. Tiplady is interesting. Between 1839 and his death in 1873 he kept a diary, extracts from which were transcribed in the nineteenth century by a man called Abram, who had been working on a history of Blackburn. The diary, a fascinating record of this significant period, then mysteriously disappeared and was only recently rediscovered – retrieved from a dustbin by Nottingham auctioneers Mellors & Kirk during a house clearance. Recently, it was transcribed by the Blackburn Local History Society, who, with the Victoria & Albert Museum in London, Blackburn Library and the Museum & Art Gallery, secured the diary for the town.

Tiplady's shop (as already said, he was a printer and bookseller) was in Church Street, near Salford Bridge. The cellar regularly flooded when the Blakewater was high, like Jo's in nearby Henry Street. A contemporary report on sanitary conditions in the town gives us an inkling as to what such a flooding brought into the building. The Blakewater is described as an elongated cesspool, 'spreading the seeds of disease and death and even contaminating the very food of the living'.

There were indeed repeated outbreaks of cholera and typhus in the town, owing to untreated sewage. In 1856 work began on a proper sewage system, but if you lived in a canal-side area you were still three times more likely to die early than in sweeter-smelling Preston New Road, where the toffs hung out. In 1858, the Blackburn Infirmary was founded by a high-profile mill-owning family by name of Pilkington. It figures in *Angels Cry Sometimes*, where Grandma Fletcher's clogs echo on the stone-flag floors and she tells Marcia, her daughter, 'I never 'ave liked the smell o' these places.' It also figures in *Looking Back* and in *Her Father's Sins*, where Queenie gives her view of the hospital in the 1950s:

> *The dampness breathed in the walls, and the wind persistently whistled through the ill-fitting window-jambs. The long snaking corridors, devoid of windows, were dark and dungeon-like. Their shadowy unclean appearance ensured that no one ever lingered in their recesses.*

Besides damp and infested conditions and poverty, poor diet also took its toll, especially on infants, more than half of whom died before their fifth birthday, just a year before they could be engaged in work. In the Lancashire coal industry in the early 1840s, boys would begin working at between six and eleven years of age. In *Don't Cry Alone*, which opens in 1868, Maisie's son, Matthew, works down the mines. He's only eleven. The younger boys were no good for heavy work and occupied positions such as door-tender. They would crouch miles underground for twelve hours a day in total darkness, until occasionally a wagon came along and the air-door had to be opened. One inspector noted that: 'Exertion there is none, nor labour, further than is requisite to open and shut a door. As these little fellows are always the youngest in the pits, I have generally found them very shy.' Less lonely a job was that of gigger, who looked after the load balance on a wagon of coal. Giggers were also amongst the youngest of the child workers down the mine.

These past weeks Maisie had been concerned about the boy. He seemed to be unusually quiet; although of course he had never been the lively little chatterbox that Cissie was. All the same, Maisie had noticed how withdrawn he'd become of late, and how he was always wanting to go to bed afore time. Lately, too, he had not been eating enough to keep a sparrow alive. She looked at him now, with his floppy mass of brown hair and eyes as violet as her own, and she thought how tender he was at eleven years old to be working alongside grown men down the mines. Not for the first time, she asked herself whether there could have been any other way she might have organised things. But the answer was always the same. When her darling man was lost in those same bloody mines, she had done the best she could; although there was never a day went by when she didn't regret the way young Matthew seemed to be paying the biggest price of all. 'Your dad would have been so proud of you, lad,' she said now in a choking voice ...

In the cotton industry, children had always helped as fetchers and carriers, as well as in the least skilled and less labour-intensive tasks. As mechanisation increased the speed and efficiency of the industry, the mill masters saw that children could take a greater part in the process. Moreover, in the cost-conscious factory system, child workers were popular because they were cheap and available. The jobs they did were often menial – such as 'scavenging', namely crawling into small and sometimes dangerous places in the machinery which would be hard to clean out otherwise –as in replacing the metal combs in the automated carding process: '. . . a hand inserted too far into the machine could result in loss of finger tips,' as Michael Winstanley writes in his excellent book, *Working Children in Nineteenth-Century Lancashire*.

It is perfectly consistent with the way the Industrial Revolution corrupted every other aspect of Nature that it should also exploit children. In the mid-eighteenth century Rousseau (in his *Discourses*, 1750 and 1755, and in *Emile* in 1762) had given authoritative expression to a long tradition of Hebrew and Christian literature that spoke of the spiritual innocence of the child and the preference of that state to that of so-called civilised man. Childhood was, as Wordsworth reiterated at the end of the eighteenth century in his long autobiographical poem 'The Prelude', the time when we are in a true state of Nature and closest to God. It was a Romantic notion over which the profit-driven mill masters were bound to ride roughshod.

Apprentices often worked for food and lodging and slept in a room in the mill or in a separate house. Commonly it was the orphaned children who suffered most from the system. A cotton apprentice-ship was a way of disposing of the 'problem' of their very existence. As young as six a lad might work twelve- to fifteen-hour shifts, which dovetailed into one another so that one clocking off would steal into the warm bed of another clocking on. Often there would be little genuine effort to bring a child on and into the more skilled areas of the industry. When a boy-apprentice became a man, he might well be laid off in favour of a younger, cheaper worker.

Conditions and standards of care created misery of Dickensian proportions. Said a mill worker in 1831, when asked how the mill masters kept the children to their work during these long, intensive hours, day after day: 'Sometimes they would tap them over the head, or nip them on the nose, or give them a pinch of snuff, or throw water in their faces . . . or shake them about to keep them waking.'

In a factory environment output was the only priority, everything and everyone yielded to that principle, and discipline could be fierce, as one twelve-year-old boy put on record in 1832: 'One time I was struck by the master on the head with his clenched fist, and kicked when I was down. I saw one girl trailed by the hair of her head, and kicked by him . . . until she roared, "Murder!" several times. There was one orphan girl who spun at the same frame with me . . . She was engaged at the mill for three years, for food and clothes. She one day got entangled in the machinery till all her clothes were torn off her back. When she was taken out, she was very much abused [by the overlooker] for letting herself get caught up.'

A contemporary report conceded that there was a serious health risk: 'These children are usually too long confined to work in close rooms, often during the night; the air they breathe from the oil, etc, employed in the machinery and other circumstances is injurious; little regard is paid to their cleanliness, and frequent changes from a warm and dense to a cold and thin atmosphere, are predisposing causes to sickness and disability . . . and has debilitated the constitution and retarded the growth of many.'

The first Factory Act (1819) prohibited employment of children under nine years of age. The Act instituted a maximum twelve-hour working day (excluding meal breaks) for children under 16, but enforcement was left to local JPs and was lax. Other Acts followed in 1833, 1844 and 1867, but in 1851, and still in 1871, more than forty per cent of all children between 10 and 14 years of age, living in Lancashire, worked, and in 1871 the county accounted for one-sixth of the nation's working boys between these ages, and nearly a quarter (22%) of all working girls in the age group. In Blackburn, as late as 1911 over 90% of all fourteen-year-olds were in employment, and 84% of all girls of that age. Further Acts raised the legal minimum working age of children to twelve years in 1901, fourteen in 1920 and sixteen in 1937.

This did not stop Jo leaving school and working in a vinegar bottling factory from the age of fourteen. 'I was allowed to leave school at fourteen because I was helping the family with a wage; you were allowed to do that.' She remembers just how fast the experience removed her childhood innocence: 'Just before leaving Blackburn I worked in a vinegar-bottling factory. There was a carrousel, one woman would put the empty vinegar bottles in, the next woman would fill them with vinegar, then one would put the tops on, I would put the labels on and some-one would take them out and crate them up and someone else would come and take the crates away. Now that place was at the foot of the road where Cicely Bridge Mill was, near the bridge. It ran down to the river, and it had these big heavy green doors, like rubber doors, you know, to run the trolleys through and out to the lorries, and the rats would come up from the river and you could be sitting doing your job with the rats running about your feet. That was my first job, and I was only there for about a month before Mum and Dad split up. But the things that I learned from those women around that carrousel. My God! I was inducted into life very quickly. A lot of that has gone into my books, things I heard, things I heard them telling each other.'

The Act of 1844 is interesting because it actually reduced the minimum working age from nine to eight in the mills, but insisted that eight- to thirteen-year-olds could only work if they also attended school – six and a half hours per day in the mills plus three hours per day (Monday to Friday only!) at school. The mill masters were allowed to dock tuppence per day from a child's wages towards the cost of schooling!

'The half-time system', as it became known, was actually the first compulsory schooling anywhere in the country, and in the context of the town's severe truancy problem the idea was touted as progressive, when, in fact, it cleverly ensured the continuance of child labour in the face of growing opposition.

'No school, no mill; no mill, no money,' was the child-workers' chant, and it was the mill's gain, not the children's.

Blackburn had as many as 6000 children in the half-time system even as late as 1875, and in 1909, in three schools monitored in Blackburn, there were still 208 half-timers out of 286 children in the twelve-to-fourteen age group.

Even when they got to school, children in the state

sector would receive only a very basic education in the 3Rs to prepare them for the mills. The mills were the focus. However bright you turned out, as one worker put it, 'them days we had to go to the mill. You weren't asked.' When, in 1870, the Blackburn School Board, dominated by mill owners, was encouraged by the Education Act to utilise ratepayers' money to start up state schools, it only ever opened four, happy to leave the business to the Church schools.

And yet, despite these appalling conditions of life, the worker poets began by exalting their sense of duty to the mill, for example by calling on operatives to work out their contracts even in the face of personal monetary loss, as in Henry Yates's dialect poem of this era, 'Never Mind 'em':

> . . . Werk yo'r contract eawt like men
> If yo've signed 'em
> If yo loyse bi th' jobs, wod then?
> Never mind 'em.
> Werk for t'best, for t'best is sure,
> Whether yo werk for t'rich or poor;
> An' if misfortunes knock at th' door,
> Never mind 'em.

Such pride and sense of duty seem extraordinary in hindsight, given the way the mill workers had been exploited and would in future years be let down.

Then, in 1862, came the worst period of depression, which really ate into the heart of the town. Jim Heyes records in *Aspects of Blackburn* that '30,000 of a population of 62,126 were receiving relief'. The figure probably underestimates the suffering, for, as local printer and bookseller Charles Tiplady noted in his diary, 'Pride made many refuse relief.'

In 1861, civil war had broken out in North America, and a blockade of the Confederate ports (the southern states, whence Blackburn's raw cotton came) prevented exports, leading to 'bad times, mass unemployment and famine' in Blackburn, even starvation.

Before the war broke out, Blackburn's mills had been over-stocked with raw fibre, and mill owners were keen to play down the risk, some feeling that articles appearing in the *Blackburn Standard* were already unsettling the workforce. Many were clearly jittery. Tiplady noted in his diary on 15 February 1861 that these were 'troublous times' and that 'a majority of hands suspended work' in the mills over a disagreement about wages.

In *Outcast*, Caleb Crowther is one of those mill owners keen to dampen speculation:

> *'There's a war brewing in America, I tell you!'*
> *The portly fellow tipped the brandy glass to his*
> *lips and drained it dry. Then, taking a chunky*
> *cigar from his top pocket, he placed it between*

his teeth and began biting on it. 'It won't be long now before Lincoln's elected to office, and, with the Republicans so intent on this anti-slavery policy, there'll be fur flying in no time. You mark my words, there'll be war on the other side of the Atlantic!'

'I hope to God you're wrong, Harrison!' declared a small, square-looking fellow seated in the deep, leather armchair by the fire, his weasel-features bathed by the heat from the flames, and his eyes most anxious as they swept the eight figures seated around the room. 'Each of us here has all our money sunk in the Lancashire cotton industry. Should there be a war in America . . . and the issue is the slaves who pick the cotton which runs our mills . . . it could mean catastrophe for Lancashire. And for every one of us here!' The thought appeared to horrify him because he was suddenly on his feet and pacing anxiously up and down.

'You're exaggerating!' protested one man.

'It's a fact though,' said another, 'it was May when Lincoln was nominated for the presidency – six months ago! And just look how the southern states have put up every obstacle to keep him from coming to office. There is strong feeling. There bloody well is! If you ask me, it's a situation which needs to be watched most carefully!'

'You're panicking, the lot of you!' intervened a bald-headed man. 'I'm telling you, there'll be no war. The cotton will be shipped in just as regularly as it's ever been and the mills of Lancashire will continue to thrive, just as they are now.' With that said, he leaned back in his chair, embracing one and all with a smug expression.

'Gentlemen.' All eyes turned to look at Caleb Crowther. So far, he had made no contribution to the debate which, since the men's departure from the dinner table to the sanctuary of the library, had become somewhat heated. Now, however, he strode to the centre of the room where he tactfully waited to ensure that he held their absolute attention. When satisfied, he continued in a sombre tone, 'The very reason you were all invited here tonight, was to discuss this matter. Of late, there has been too much talk of what's happening in America and it's time to put an end to it!' Here his vivid eyes pausing, he oppressively scrutinized each of his guests in turn, and each was visibly affected. 'Isn't it enough that the Blackburn Standard puts out such articles that have our very mill-hands stopping their work to air their views and spread even more unrest? It's up to us . . . the owners . . . to set an example! If we show ourselves to be affected by unfounded gossip and trouble-

some rumours, then how the devil are we to
expect any different from the fools we employ?'
Though his expression was one of fury, his
voice was remarkably calm. 'I say there will be
no war in America. The slaves will pick the
cotton as they always have, and the people of
Lancashire will go on processing it in our mills.
There is no place here for scaremongers!'

Soon, however, the American Civil War and its
implications for Blackburn were apparent. Mills
began short-term working, some factories closed,
and somehow, as Tiplady recorded on 16 November
1861, even the weather conspired to depress: 'First
fall of snow this Winter – heavy, followed by a keen
frost – time fairly gloomy; work scarce; cotton dear;
money bad to get.'

The town set up a Central Relief Committee, and
on 20 January 1862, Tiplady wrote: 'Great distress
in consequence of the American War. A soup kitchen
established in the Town.'

The soup kitchen was in fact on Cleaver Street,
where '2400 quarts of soup were dispensed each
day; meal and bread on alternate days.' On 5 March,
Tiplady noted, 'Heavy fall of snow. The distress of
the Operatives continues; and relief is afforded to
thousands of unemployed poor.'

In *Outcast*, bargee Marlow Tanner tells her sister,
Sal, of the indignity of the very needy:

173

*'I don't need to tell you, Sal ... you know
well enough. You've seen them ... in the soup
queues. And you've seen the boarded-up houses
where folks have been thrown out because they
can't pay the rent. We at least have some work,
and we have a roof over our heads.'*

There had been need of a soup kitchen before, in the
1840s, and Beattie records that in 1826 and again in
1847 a visitor system had had to be organised to
rescue the truly starving – public officers winkling
out the worst hit – but 1862 would be Blackburn's
nadir, its worst depression, and, finally, the town
began to prepare itself:

*The newly elected Mayor of Blackburn, Mr
R. H. Hutchinson, had anticipated that great
distress and trouble would manifest itself in the
coming winter. To this end, it had been agreed
that the sum of two hundred pounds would be
set aside for distribution to the growing number
of needy by the clergy and ministers of the
town. But, meanwhile, a meeting of the textile
manufacturers had resulted in the drastic step
of closing down even more establishments, the
consequence of which was to throw an even
greater number of operatives into the ever-
increasing ranks of the unemployed. Not a man
was safe in his work and though Emma's heart*

bled for those families already living in fear, she also felt desperately concerned for her husband. Gregory Denton was a changed man. Whereas he had once gone to work of a morning with a spring in his step and a warm kiss for Emma, he now left without a word of farewell and with his face gravely serious. His stooped figure went down the street as though he was approaching the hangman rather than his place of work.

Contemporary poets refer to 1861, the start of the American Civil War, as the onset of the 'Cotton Panic'. So many were inspired to verse in this period that John Baron coined their work 'Poetry of the Panic'.

William Billington, born in Samlesbury in 1827, was pre-eminent in this 'school' and at various times 'a doffer, a stripper and grinder, a weaver and a taper'. A doffer removes and replaces bobbins from spinning machines, a stripper empties bobbins of unused thread, which is sent for waste, and a taper minds a dry taping machine. There are many uses for a grinder, but none specific to the textile industry.

Being poor, Billington was educated at Sunday School, though later he attended classes at the Mechanics' Institution in Blackburn. His lot, like Jo's, was '. . . cast amid the lowly masses':

Whose joy and sorrows I full oft have sung
And through the glooms which cloud the
working classes
Some feeble gleams of sunshine may have flung.

Two volumes by Billington, 'Sheen and Shade' and 'Lancashire Songs', were published twenty-two years apart, in 1861 and 1883, due to the fact that the people of Blackburn were too poor to buy books in the intervening years. His two poems, 'Blackburn as It Is' and 'The Cry of the Crowd' breathe the very spirit of lament that characterised the human contours of the town at this time. Writing from personal experience, not blighted by intellectual or any other pretension, he finds his way unimpeded to the point:

I have battled with Want
For a terrible term,
And been silent, till silence seemed crime,
Yet I mean not to rant,
But will yield you a germ
Of plain truth in an unpolished rhyme . . .

Want bound people together in the seemingly impossible task of survival. Marcia may be talking of the 1930s' depression in *Angels Cry Sometimes*, but the point is just as valid for the 1860s:

It had often struck her that desperate need, for all its horrors, had a strange way of binding folks together, increasing their appreciation of one another and, as a result, there had emerged a kinship between the folk hereabout that was strong and comforting. They were a hard-living courageous folk, whose profound strength and faith helped them to live each day as it came, to forge new friendship and to cherish the old. If one suffered, they all suffered.

Poverty itself was exalted and given a place of respect in this period, as in 'The Honest Poor', a poem by Hugh Gardiner Graham, a Scotsman by birth, but resident in Blackburn from 1863, this period of terrible depression:

There's honour in the poor man's breast more
*   dear to him than gold;*
There's loving kindness in his heart; there's truth
*   and courage bold . . .*
There's resolution in his soul to brave life's
*   toilsome way . . .*

By 1902, however, the dichotomy of the wealthy mill owner and his impoverished worker was painfully evident to the workforce, and in that year, when George Hull is making Henry Yates's poem, 'Never Mind 'em', part of his collection, he is able to declare that there are very few operatives left in Blackburn who would work out their contracts in the face of monetary loss.

Stripped of his autonomy, independence and tradition, cast into poverty and misery to make a handful of mill owners rich, the Blackburn weaver was finally beginning to lay duty aside and speak out, as here, in William Billington's seminal poem, 'Fraud, The Evil of the Age':

> *With what unutterable shame and scorn,*
> *Humiliation and indignant rage,*
> *The bosom of the honest man is torn*
> *Who contemplates the evils of this age.*

CHAPTER FOUR

Betrayed

So, what took the working man so long to speak up? Given the poverty and degradation into which so many fell in the nineteenth century, why didn't the Blackburn cotton-worker flex his muscles about poor wages and living and working conditions earlier? Why was it, after the hand-loom workers failed to halt the mechanisation of the industry, Blackburn became, in Derek Beattie's words, 'one of the most peaceful of weaving towns right up to 1914'?

The story of how the mill masters got away with so much is tragic because it turns on the exploitation, painstakingly deliberate, of the heroic, resolute, un-yielding character that we have associated with the tradition of Blackburn spinners and weavers since the beginning, a character which, as their fate un-folded before them, kept many obdurately optimistic until the end.

Far from there being a 'them and us' mentality in Blackburn in the nineteenth century, there was a 'one of us' mentality, deliberately encouraged by a mill-owner's understanding and manipulation of the tradition from which their workers' characters came. Perversely, the mill owners understood the tradition because it was their tradition too.

Right from the start the revolution was master-minded by ordinary people, who, like the domestic hand-loom workers, were of the land. The Manor of Blackburn ceased to be in the hands of the aristocracy in 1721, after Thomas Belasyse Viscount Falconbergh sold out to three men who came originally of yeoman stock (freeholder families of common, not aristocratic birth) – William Baldwin, Henry Feilden and William Sudell. By and by, Baldwin sold out to the Feildens, who, with the Sudells, became instrumental in the transformation of the Blackburn cotton industry.

In 1798, Henry Sudell had more hand-loom operatives working for him than anyone in the area, and called the tune for all merchant manufacturers, who had to match or undercut his terms or lose their operatives to him. But no one would be immune from risk in the industrialisation of the world, however early in its inception, and in 1827 Sudell fell from millionaire to bankrupt after a failed foreign speculation. So the Feildens swallowed him up, too. There is still a pub, close to the original base of the Sudells, north of Blackburn at Mellor Brook, called The Feilden's Arms.

The Feildens lived to the west of Blackburn at Witton Park, and with sole control of the Manor they went from strength to strength, continuing to own some two thousand acres of Blackburn into the 1880s and dispensing their largesse by founding the local technical college, re-establishing the sixteenth-century Queen Elizabeth's Grammar School, and, as we have already seen, by granting Blackburn the fifty-acre Corporation Park.

These families had been small freeholders. They could relate to the rural values of their workers. Moreover, not only were they of the land, but once they had made their money, they returned to it, and in this they set the mould for mill owners of the future.

Typically, as a mark of his success, a mill owner would move out of town and emulate the life of the rural squire. Indeed this whole squirearchical theme permeated the cotton-mill scene. For, just as the village squire owned the lives of his villagers, so the mill owner owned the lives of his factory operatives. In Blackburn, as indeed in many rural squirearchies throughout the nation, it worked well, without resentment, everyone knowing their place.

In the early days, the owners came from the ranks of merchants who had facilitated the domestic weaving system. Unlike the putter-out, the merchant's contacts and buying-and-selling expertise had not been made redundant by the mechanisation of industry. Eventually, others with an eye to the main chance, men with genuine working-class status, came up through the industry to join them. They found their feet despite not having the merchants' ready money because, at the start, it wasn't a capital-intensive business. Machine manufacturers were only too happy to extend generous terms of credit in order to establish themselves.

Leonard Horner, a factory inspector, writes in 1837 about a mill owner called Horsfield who had risen from the working classes and made a fortune of £300,000, which most certainly was a fortune in those days, but couldn't write his own name: 'He told me that at 18 years of age [in the late 1780s] he had not five shillings in the world beyond his weekly wages of 15 shillings. Out of his wages he saved £28, bought a spinning jenny and made £30 the first year. In 1831 he made £24,000 of profit. He employs 1200 people. He is not a solitary case; there are many not unlike him in this part of the country.'

Gradually there arose an in-crowd, mill-owner scene, a club whose members took over positions of power in the town, the best of them managing to do this while giving the impression of still being one of the people. Money was not enough in itself to ensure membership of the club. Derek Beattie tells how the brewer Daniel Thwaites was at one time Blackburn's richest man, but he remained an outsider, a nonmember of the in-crowd club, even after he became an MP.

It was of course a cotton club. You had to be in cotton. You also had to have money, but not shout about it. New-money arrogance and pretension would not win you membership. You also had to evince, or at least indulge, the character of 'a gradely mon' – honest, straight and fair, stoical principle, pride in your work, for that was what gained you respect with the workers and ensured a loyal power base.

Harry Hornby was both a full member of the club and a Blackburn MP for a long period up to 1910. As Beattie writes: 'Hornby typified the kind of man that the people of Blackburn admired and looked up to. He was known locally as "Mr Harry", the "owd 'un" or "the gam' cock". He personified the qualities most respected in Blackburn society. He had little knowledge of affairs outside the borough ... yet when necessary he knew just what he stood for and stuck to his beliefs.'

When a mill owner like Hornby stood for office, he sought support not where he lived, but in the area of his mill, amongst his people. Beattie tells of cotton workers pinning the colours of their master to their machines. Worker loyalty to the mill was akin to football fan and club. A team spirit was encouraged by inter-mill games of football, brass bands and the like. Looking for comparison today, one thinks of the twentieth-century anthemic culture of corporate Japan. Workers and mill owners in Blackburn shared the same values, the same work ethic, they shared the same tradition . . . *didn't they?*

Binding this supposed shared loyalty was a 'Blackburn against the world' philosophy, for what happened outside Blackburn had no relevance at all. There was a carefully worked, inward-looking focus on your mill, your street, your pub. Also, the town's insularity was celebrated in a kind of political *omerta* in Westminster, a tradition of silence amongst Blackburn MPs. They simply would not speak. Harry Hornby managed never to utter a single word in Parliament in twenty-three years as a backbencher. Memories scored with recent images of Blackburn politicians – Barbara Castle, Jack Straw (who is not in fact of the area) – may find this scarcely credible. The strategy sealed Blackburn off from distracting influences and encouraged indifference to what was going on outside, the divisive them-and-us mentality that characterised the industrial scene elsewhere.

This hold that mill owners exercised over the working classes brought about an overwhelmingly Conservative workforce. Tiplady became Chairman of the Blackburn Operative Conservative Association and his 1839 Annual Statement evinces a widespread feeling amongst workers: 'At this period of time there is no need of lengthened argument to demonstrate the vast importance of Societies like ours, whether to the members thereof, as furnishing them with a shield against the dangerous theories and seductive mischief of falsely-called "Liberalism", or to the community at large, attending to preserve a sound heart and an honest spirit in those who are the very thews and sinews of our State – the upright, industrious, independent artisans of Britain.'

So noticeable was worker compliance that as late as 1900, the Blackburn Tory party was accused of buying votes 'by means of the beer barrel'. Clearly, pressure was exerted at various levels. For example, the Blackburn poet and grocer Robert Clemesha had his rent increased by £15 a year by his landlord, John Fleming, upon discovering that he did not intend to vote Tory at the time of the 1832 Reform Bill.

The Second Reform Act, in 1867, increased the number of Blackburn voters by a factor of five, but the new electorate, swelled by the working class, happily voted in a Tory.

So marked was the Tory allegiance in the workforce by 1932 that Oswald Mosley selected Blackburn to launch his British Union of Fascists, marching through the town with his black-shirted followers, believing the workers to be susceptible to coercion from the far Right. But he had misread the tenor. Blackburn spinners and weavers were not Right-wing extremists. What guided them was their tradition, a resolute work ethic and sense of duty, a tradition that came from way back. They no more belonged to the loony Right than the loony Left. They were apolitical. What they stood for were their ideals, which the mill masters shared ... *didn't they?*

Even into the twentieth century in Blackburn, long after William Billington wrote 'Fraud, The Evil of the Age', and even after the bleakest depressions of the 1920s and '30s, there was endless optimism that things would get better; endless resolve amongst the mill workers. William Woodruff shakes his head sadly, but in awe, at his father, forced out of work by industrial depression, trailing off each morning to nearby towns, avoiding men that would beat him up for being a 'knobstick' (a strike-breaker) and joining crowds in the hope of being taken on. Woodruff's sister, Brenda, was less charitable, referring to him as 'a gaumless creature. He had the head and brains of a brass knob. He didn't foresee anything because he never thought about anything. He was a grand worker, nobody better, but where brains were concerned he was lost.'

Woodruff, like millions of others, could not imagine himself outside the class into which tradition confined him – 'confined' because, sadly, his tradition had ceded autonomy and independence, the right to think for oneself, though the need to do so became increasingly clear. When finally the workers cried 'Fraud' as they watched the wealthy mill owners retreating to their country houses, their concept of 'duty' – Owd Peter 'ne'er his duty shirk'd' – changed acrimoniously to a demand for 'rights!', a position we have yet to get beyond.

There is, throughout Jo's *oeuvre*, a sense of this duty, though often it comes with one leaving another their duty to perform. In *Looking Back*, Molly Tattersall gives up her fiancé, Alfie Craig, to look after her six brothers and sisters when her mother leaves her father. In *Her Father's Sins*, Queenie realises she will 'have to grow up quickly in order to take care of Aunt Biddy', and when Biddy dies, her sense of duty extends to cleaning up her father's drunken vomit and generally looking after him, finally to be raped by him. In *Born to Serve*, Elizabeth Marshall recognises a duty to love the child who is saying that she is pregnant by her father.

For men, work was seen as a duty first; only later was it deemed a right. It was demoralising to be put out of work as well as materially impoverishing. In *Tomorrow the World*, Silas Little, the best tailor in Blackburn, believes that responsibility binds us all, and 'the only way we can survive is by learning to love it as if it were part of our very soul.' Silas learns to love it so well that he dies working late into the night at his table.

Jo herself rose to a sense of duty when she and her brothers and sisters were consigned to the Council Home. Later, like Kelly's friend Amy in *Somewhere, Someday*, who takes responsibility for her siblings,

Jo recognised and rose again to her family responsibilities when her pregnant mother left her father and took Jo and her sisters with her.

The nineteenth-century mill masters did all they could to affirm and encourage these ideals, traditional principles and values, which, to their great advantage, placed pride in one's work and duty dead centre, and gave the worker, if not much money, hard-won dignity and self-respect.

Thereafter, theirs was a strategy of non-adversarial management, of pre-empting worker strife, of implementing reforms that cost nothing and gave the distinct impression that they cared. For example, vigorous support of legislation limiting child working hours pre-empted a more far-reaching factory-reform lobby, which occurred elsewhere, but not in Blackburn, in the 1830s.

A decade or so later, unions would start to form, as Maisie notes in *Don't Cry Alone*:

She had been interested to hear how unions for ordinary workers were springing up all over the country. 'It won't last though,' she told Beth cynically. 'You'll see ... the high and mighty buggers in government won't let ordinary folks have no say in nothing.' Maisie harboured no illusions where men in tall hats and carrying canes were concerned. 'They're all mouth and bloody trousers ... don't know what it's like

*to go without a crust, or to have their bellies
rumbling with hunger, or to lie in a damp bed
and watch a cockroach crawl up the wall and
on to the ceiling where it might fall on yer face
in the middle of the night. What the bleedin'
hell do they know, eh? What do they know of
ordinary folk such as you and me?'*

The mill masters became past masters at avoiding confrontation with the unions. They gained positions on committees and organisations pressing for
change, eventually to control them. They instituted
the Standard List – standard rates of pay for all jobs
throughout all the mills in Blackburn – thereby
removing a key platform of union power. In 1834,
the year when six farmworkers were sentenced to
seven years' penal servitude for forming a trade union
in a village called Tolpuddle in Dorset (the Tolpuddle
Martyrdom was a key event in trade-union history)
the Blackburn mill masters actually joined forces
with their workers over the New Poor Law.

The law was a milestone in a series of Acts
designed to relieve poverty, but it turned on the
principle that relief should not be so benevolent
as to encourage people not to work. 'Every penny
bestowed that tends to render the condition of the
pauper more eligible than that of the independent
labourer is a bounty on indolence and vice,' argued
the commissioners with something of a modern ring.

Fear of the workhouse was palpable, and Blackburn poet William Gaspey railed in his poetry against the 'Modern Star-Chamber', which the Poor Law legislation set up. In 'The Victim' he denounces the law for making the mother – not the father – responsible for the maintenance of an illegitimate child, summoning support for his theme with the heart-rending image of a pauper 'in the convulsive agonies of death', shielding 'her infant from the cutting blast' and calling with her last breath, 'God protect my child!' For nobody else would . . . except the Blackburn mill masters . . . *wouldn't they?*

Elsewhere, beyond Blackburn, townships set about herding the unemployed into workhouses, splitting up families at the door, making life for the unemployed as unpleasant as possible, and driving a wedge between society and the unemployed. Poverty was for the first time a stigma, by law. But in Blackburn, aware how strong feelings were running, the mill masters seized the opportunity to further their all-for-one-and one for-all philosophy. They openly flouted the new law, continuing to extend relief to impoverished families outside the workhouse system, and the strategy put them in good stead to deal with the first big test of master–worker solidarity, which came between 1838 and 1850, when the Chartists made a national rallying call to the new industrial working class.

A charter for social equality was drawn up at national level. Electoral reform was touted as the first step to securing it. Universal suffrage was one of its six principles and came in response to the Reform Bill of 1832, which had merely given votes to the middle class.

Support was strong in the Midlands and the North, but in Blackburn, disarmed by the mill masters' recent opposition to the New Poor Law, the mill workers paid little heed. A call to strike in 1839 was ignored completely, and the *Blackburn Standard* praised Blackburn workers for their '*co-operative spirit*' and for the value they attached to the 'spirit of industry'.

In 1842, however, there were problems, though it is instructive to see how they came about. 'On 6th August,' Tiplady writes in his diary 'commenced one of the most extraordinary and complete turnouts which has ever occurred in this Kingdom; it began at Stapley Bridge, on a question of wages relative to a proposed deduction of 2d for cash from the most unprincipled Master connected with the Anti-Corn Law League. [The Anti-Corn Law League was an organisation founded in 1839 to oppose the restriction of foreign imports made legal by the Corn Laws.] This deduction was attempted at a time when the Trade, which had been depressed [was making] a healthy revival, and so exasperated the Operatives that they refused to go to work altogether.'

On 15 August, Tiplady records that the rioting workers were prevented from entering a mill by:

... a detachment of the 72nd Highlanders under the command of Lieut. Col. Arbuthnot. Fifteen prisoners were taken ... In the meanwhile straggling gangs of ten or twelve took the advantage of surprising different Mills in the Town and with the exception of about four the whole were closed before night. Foiled in the general attempts ... the mob retired for the day and threatened a descent of more violent and determined characters on the following morning. Accordingly, they appeared in great strength on the Accrington Road and proceeded to the Magistrates having installed a strong police force with a company of the 72nd Highlanders, a troop of the Lancashire Yeomanry Corps and Troops of the 11th Hussars to meet them. They encountered the mob at Further Gate ... pursuing them across the fields in every direction. In the course of a few moments they were utterly dispersed and about 75 Prisoners captured, which were lodged in the Barracks for safety.

By such vigilant means the Town and Neighbourhood was saved from pillage and other violations of the Law – yet on the following day the soldiers were obliged to fire on the mob, and several persons were severely wounded, but happily not mortally.

Beattie reports that eleven strikers were transported to Tasmania and some fifty-eight sent to prison. According to Tiplady, the uprising occurred when a foolish mill master demanded a wage reduction for political purpose and at a time when business was good. That had been the fatal tactical mistake, but the riot would not have been so serious if the force of Blackburn workers had not been swelled by incoming Chartist strikers from Manchester and Stalybridge. It is unlikely that they will have been especially welcome. Certainly, not much more was heard of Chartism in Blackburn henceforth.

Worker riots were, indeed, unusual in the town, as was the use of force to quell unrest. A more typical response from the resourceful industrialists came in 1845, when mill owners sorted out a demo by treating one thousand activists to tea.

This unique management–worker relationship was largely maintained until late in the nineteenth century when takeovers and amalgamations of mills began to dilute worker loyalty to one master, and the mill masters themselves began to retreat to their mansions on the fringe of the town, leaving a new, lower middle-class managerial level to administer their businesses for them. This engendered resentment: the new men were not looked up to in quite the same way as those who had forged the Industrial Revolution in the first place. These were pen-pushers, not hands-on entrepreneurs. Heroes were made of more adventurous stuff.

What had riveted the 'spirit of industry' into the hearts of the workers had disappeared. It was no longer 'one for all and all for one'. Their fellow travellers had deserted them, the masters had used their ticket out. Suddenly, the gulf between 'them' and 'us' was made clear. This is the period that produced William Billington's worker-awareness poem, 'Fraud, The Evil of the Age', previously quoted. The mill masters had been rumbled, but what could the workers do about it?

The answer came in May 1878. Following an insensitive wage cut of ten per cent, 20,000 of them came out on strike. A crowd of 5000 ran riot from Blackburn to Clayton Manor in Wilpshire, the house of Colonel Robert Raynsford Jackson, Chairman of the Textile Employers' Federation. He and his family managed to escape in a brougham, but the house was fired and gutted – damage to the tune of £12,000 was caused – and the rioters dragged a burned-out four-wheeled carriage back to Blackburn as a trophy. The following day the windows of sixty-four houses in middle-class Preston New Road were smashed. Troops were called out and the workers' leader, a man called Smalley, was sentenced to fifteen years of penal servitude. There were eight other jail sentences

– from eight to fifteen years. It was a humiliating defeat, and deepened the sense of worker enslavement.

Twelve years later, Blackburn's Chamber of Commerce warned of the dangers of the town having only one string to its bow – cotton. Blackburn would stand or fall with the cotton industry, and there were worrying signs of it doing the latter.

After the First War (1914–18) there was a short-lived mini-boom, but in the 1920s and '30s the downward spiral began, and it was dramatic. Foreign competitors had used the war to supply Blackburn's traditional markets, and, in a clear display of loss of control at the helm, Blackburn sold them the machinery to do it. Crucial to the industry had been exports to India of Blackburn Greys. Between 1913 and 1936 these exports were reduced by more than eighty per cent. By the 1920s, India, China and Japan had snaffled Blackburn's trade for themselves. Unable to obtain Blackburn cloth during the war, India had looked to its own industry, and Blackburn had actually sold them the machines to tool up, the town's Technical College proudly training overseas students in the textile skills in which it specialised.

In *The Road to Nab End*, William Woodruff writes of the hunger and poverty in Blackburn following the Crash of 1920, of his father, in desperation, taking in mail bags to sew and mending clogs.

The day his father scrubbed the Victoria monument in Blackburn he describes as the bleakest of the Great Depression. Under the National Insurance Act of 1920, Woodruff's father received fifteen shillings a week for fifteen weeks, his mother five shillings for a shorter period. There were also benefits from the trade union, but they soon ran out.

Between 1918 and 1922 the number of looms in operation was cut by a half. A partial recovery in 1924–25 was followed by the General Strike in 1926, abandoned eight days later. Humiliation and victimisation ensued under the auspices of the Trade Disputes and Trade Union Act of 1927, which abolished rights fought for and won by the workers earlier. In 1929 the spinners were locked out to enforce wage reductions. In 1930 it was the weavers' turn. By then half the workers in Blackburn were on the streets. In the period 1930–38 the number of unemployed veered between 21.5% and 47% in the town, and underemployment was as much of a problem. Hidden by these figures, bad as they were, was the fact that the cotton industry operated on a piece-work basis. Men were working, and therefore not classified as unemployed, but were not earning enough to live.

The output of industry had been halved since 1914 and the number of workers reduced by nine-tenths since before the war. Late in 1931 the cotton industry in Blackburn reached the point of collapse:

'Father was smashing looms with a sledgehammer which he had earlier tuned with all the skill of a piano-tuner,' writes Woodruff.

When Mahatma Gandhi, the Indian political and spiritual leader and social reformer, visited England for political talks in the same year, he was invited to Blackburn to see for himself the misery that his industrial policy, which had banned cloth imports from Britain, was causing. *The Lancet*, the British journal of the medical profession, reported that people in Blackburn were literally dying of starvation. Gandhi, with experience of worse poverty in India, was not impressed. 'The poverty I have seen distresses me,' he was quoted as saying, 'but compared to the poverty and pauperism of the starving millions of India, the poverty of Lancashire dwindles into insignificance.' In October of the following year, 1932, a hunger march to London was given a rousing send-off in the market square.

This, then, was the situation that met Jo's parents when they arrived in Derwent Street and started a family. Jo's mother claimed to remember Mahatma Gandhi's visit. 'Gandhi killed it off. Mum said, "That's Gandhi's fault, all our cotton mills closing." He bought all the machines.' There is mention of his visit in both *Let Loose the Tigers* and *Angels Cry Sometimes*.

CHAPTER FIVE

The Full, Vicious Circle

The economy of the town depended on cotton. Cotton dominated everything, and when cotton failed, there was little for anyone to turn to. The 1930s did see one or two alternative moves to stem the widespread depression. In 1936, Blackburn's first industrial estate started up, an electronics firm its first tenant, and the Thwaites family brewery (founded in 1797, the name pronounced without the 'h'), and Dutton's, another of the town's brewers, both hung in there. But nothing could take up the slack left by cotton. By 1937 the number of power looms had been reduced to 37% of the boom-time total. The number rose a little after the Second War, when there was again a mini-boom, and then steadily declined from 1956 onwards.

During this period, however, there were some improvements nationally. In 1942 the Beveridge Report determined to make 'want under any circumstances unnecessary' and laid out the basis of a social-security system. In 1948 the National Health Service was set up to be financed mainly by taxation. By then, typhoid and cholera had been stamped out. The medics had as good as got rid of that other scourge, rickets, and the death rate from tuberculosis was being lowered year on year.

Still, however, in the 1940s and '50s and right up to the '60s there was no bathroom or indoor toilet in forty per cent of Blackburn homes, whereas in Manchester, just a few miles to the south, 200 acres of the worst slums had already been cleared by 1939. 'We built blocks of flats on the cleared sites, which not long before had been teeming slums,' reported the Manchester Council in 1947, noting advisedly, 'but building on old slum sites cuts two ways. Though the flats are new, the districts are old and overcrowded, as many people had to live in the new flats as used to live in the old slums. You do not always improve things by cramming people in layers on top of one another instead of spreading them out sideways with more space.'

This was not a lesson Blackburn learned immediately. The town's two-decade clearance plan included the replacement of Larkhill with the tower blocks still in evidence today and brought a cry for a stay of execution from townspeople, who didn't want their terraced-house communities destroyed. In *Her Father's Sins*, Rick Marsden's father has an interest in the post-war slum clearance programme in Blackburn. The programme was halted for a while and the overall strategy modified to include grants for renovation of existing dwellings, but Jo's Derwent Street community was laid waste, and Henry Street disappeared in a wholesale clearance and rebuild of the town centre. Plans were unveiled to take down the clock tower and cover the market with a new shopping precinct in 1955, at the very moment that her mum took the family into exile.

By then, the so-called 'spirit of industry' was all but dead. Millions had been made and lost and salted away. The workers had been well and truly done.

One can talk of tradition and of the character of the northern working class, obdurate in the face of the big rip-off, and too easily forget that the revolution broke many a family and drove more to drink. At the lowest end of Blackburn society, character was constantly degraded by a combination of poor education, want and drink, even from the start. In 1835, the vicar of Blackburn, Reverend John Whittaker, wrote of the Blackburn underclass: 'Their immorality in every respect, their gross, filthy habits, their ruffian-like brutality beggar all description. The Sabbath breaking and drunkenness are dreadful. The beer shops have increased the latter to a frightful extent.' The chaplain of Preston prison could only agree: 'There is a greater proportion of the uneducated classes in Blackburn than in Preston and the passion for liquor is a source of ruin and disgrace . . .'

By 1862 there was one drink outlet for every twenty-three houses in Blackburn. 'Do you wonder that most people tried to forget the long hours of work and the misery of their homes by going to the only places of warmth and amusement, the taverns and gin palaces?' questioned one observer. Jo writes in *Her Father's Sins* that ninety years on, 'It was an undisputed fact – which any real red-blooded Lancastrian would relate with chest-bursting pride – that there were more pubs, under the colourful names of Bells, Brown Cows, Navigations, and Jug and Bottles, than there were shops.' But the effect this had on life at home was dreadful, as seven-year-old Queenie saw:

Queenie looked around the room. By the look of it, she thought George Kenney's cronies must have turned up with more booze after she'd gone to sleep. Strewn from one end of the oil-cloth to the other, empty bottles and jugs had trickled their last sediments into small pools of dark brown stain. There wasn't an ornament left standing upright anywhere on the side-board, and somebody's half-hearted attempt at poking the fire had filled the hearth with black cinders and ash, like a thick dirt carpet.

Over by the scullery door, the stand-chair

which normally stood there like a dutiful sentry was toppled over in a most undignified manner. Queenie surmised that some drunken body had made a futile attempt at diving for the back door which led to the outer yard. Futile, because of the considerable deposit of reeking vomit, spread across the chair-legs and surrounding oilcloth.

Queenie had become used to clearing up such a mess.

Drunkenness only relieved the problem of want and dire exploitation when it ended in unconsciousness. Otherwise, and when consciousness returned, it exacerbated it, and caused most of the crime in the town from 1830 on, so that publicans (and licensing hours) became the favourite quarry of officers of the law.

On 31 January 1856, a publican called William Durham complained of being 'dogged like an assassin, hunted and watched like a felon', in a letter to the *Blackburn Standard*:

Sir – Some startling outrages – personal attacks with violence – have very recently been committed . . . between Sunday night and Monday morning, rows of streets were visited by a roving set of blackguards, gardens trampled upon, trees uprooted, shutters broken, knockers

*wrenched off, and such works of wanton
destruction completed as must have occupied
the perpetrators a considerable length of time;
and all this done without the detection of a
single offender. Where were the police? They
were looking after the publicans and beer-
sellers, playing at hide and seek in sly corners
and dark entries and obscure alleys; crouched
in back-yards and behind doors, ready to spring
upon the unwary ale seller and spirit vendors,
for the smallest infraction of the Law.*

It is difficult not to see the huge number of pubs in
the town as the final solution in the pacification and
exploitation of the workers, for the mill masters
owned many of these watering holes and rarely built
them beyond the mill-worker colonies. In the enslavement process of the Blackburn working man,
drink was the effective lobotomy. Tragically, because
drink does not relieve humiliation, and because pubs
were a male preserve and drinking got bound up
with the hard-working, macho element in the working man's character, it came to have a terrible effect
on the community, and in particular, as Mary Jane
Brindle discovered, on Blackburn women, when the
working man's resentment at his lot was turned on
his own family.

'In Blackburn,' wrote J. Corin in *Mating,
Marriage & the Status of Women*, published in 1910,

'it is the usual thing for the husband, when he comes home late at night, to give his wife a kicking and beating. The women take it as part of the daily round and don't complain.' The tragic reverberations of this sort of scene are still to be found today. The legend, pointedly printed on a set of beer mats sitting on the bar of a pub opposite Burnley police station, reads: 'Last year over 18,500 people contacted Lancashire police to report cases of domestic violence.'

There can be no better justification for Jo's preoccupation with family violence, as seen from the child's point of view in *Somewhere, Someday*, where Kelly Wilson recalls a birthday party in Johnson Street, only a few streets away from where Jo lived:

'It was my tenth birthday. Mam had made me a wonderful party,' Kelly began. 'Mam baked the cake and dressed it with candles, and all the neighbours came.' Her voice broke with emotion. 'He said I wasn't to have a party, that it was a bloody nuisance.'

She smiled, a sad, childish smile. 'They fought for days . . . like they fought about everything she wanted to do.'

Her eyes widened in surprise. 'Somehow she managed to persuade him. He didn't stay, though. He went to the pub. "I won't be back till it's over!" he said, and to be truthful,

I didn't want him there. He always spoiled things.'

'At least you got yer party.' Poor as her childhood was, Amy thanked the Lord she had never suffered in the way Kelly had suffered.

'It was the best party ever,' Kelly said softly. *'We laughed and played, and everyone was having a wonderful time. Mam lit the candles on my cake and I couldn't blow them all out at once.'* She chuckled then. *'Lenny Parker got excited and blew them all out instead. I didn't really mind, but his mam clouted him round the ear and threatened to take him home if he didn't behave himself.'*

A change of mood came over her as she recalled what happened next.

'He came back early, drunk as a lord. "I want this lot out of here," he yelled, and began throwing things about. The children were crying and everyone knew he was out for trouble. In minutes they were all gone; except me and our mam.'

'What about your brother?'

Kelly sighed. *'Michael hid in the scullery as usual.'* Reliving the day, she described it in every detail. *'When he began swiping things off the table and smashing them against the wall, Mam shouted for Michael to take me out.'* In her mind's eye it was as real as the day it *happened, over thirty years ago.* 'As we ran through the scullery door, I saw him! He grabbed our mam by the hair and fought her to the ground. I screamed for Michael to help her, but he seemed to be frozen.'

Pausing to take a breath, Kelly wondered if she could go on. It was too real, too alive in her mind.

She heard Amy's voice, soft and persuasive. 'Don't keep it inside,' she said. 'There's just you and me here, no one else.'

Knowing she could trust her, Kelly went on. 'It had been raining all day, and was still coming down heavy,' she said. 'The yard and cellar were flooded ankle-high as always. Anyway, Michael took me down the steps as far as we could go, and there we sat.' *She shivered.* 'It was cold, too. The rain soaked us to the skin, but we couldn't go back inside. We daren't.' *Closing her eyes, she could hear it all.* 'My father was like a crazy thing. We could hear him shouting, things being thrown about, and our mam . . . oh, dear God, she sounded terrified. We could hear her cries, "Don't . . . please don't".' *Here Kelly's voice broke.* 'I tried to break away from Michael, but he held me fast, so all I could do was call out to my father. "Leave her alone!" I yelled, over and over. But he took no notice.'

When she faltered, Amy urged, 'Go on, Kelly.'

'Suddenly it all went quiet. We heard the key click in the back door, then a sound from inside, like furniture being shuffled about. I remember Michael telling me to stay where I was, and not to move until he came for me.' *Frowning, she momentarily closed her eyes, reading the pictures in her mind. 'He went to the top step and stood on tiptoes, looking through the window. I heard him shout out, then he was banging his fists on the door. "Open this door! Let me in or I'll break it down!" I'd never seen him so agitated. Suddenly the door gave beneath his weight and he was in. "Stay where you are, Kelly!" he yelled. Because I was afraid and confused, I did as I was told.'* *Putting her hands over her ears, she said, 'I sat very still, with my eyes closed and my hands like this, and I waited.'*

On *Desert Island Discs*, Jo told Sue Lawley: 'The book has exaggerated what happened. But my father did come home on Fridays and there were arguments and they were bad and it did upset the children.' But what actually happened between Barney and Mary is not the only issue. As we have seen, it was a problem many families suffered; it was a point on an emotional barometer reached for any or all of the reasons discussed. The very fact that the pattern of drink and violence was taken for granted is the point, and it is out of that that so much of Jo's fiction springs. The women take the violence as part of the daily round and don't complain.

In *Living a Lie*, set in the 1970s and '80s, Mildred Marsh berates her brother for beating his wife, Lucinda. All Lucinda had wanted was 'a love as deep and loyal as hers'. In desperation she throws herself under a train, attempting to take her daughter with her.

'Lucinda Marsh was never a tart. She was too attractive for her own good, yes, and she was like a kid at heart. She hated arguments and fighting. She wanted nothing more than to be a good mother and wife, and you made her suffer for it. She was the minnow and you were the shark. You took advantage of her soft nature . . . used her as though she was your personal property. You showed her off to your cronies, then slapped her good and hard if they dared to look at her in a certain way.'

'You don't know what you're talking about.'

'Well, now, that's where you're wrong. Lucinda came to me time and again after you'd beaten her up. She was desperately unhappy, yet still she adored you . . . begged me not to confront you.'

She spat out her next words. 'If any man treated me like you treated her, I'd cut his balls off while he slept!'

It is not chance that Mildred threatens the man's virility. Worker pride and a sense of honour could easily become warped and transformed into egotism in the face of exploitation and humiliation. Pride is a quiet strength, stoical, heroic even. The egotist, on the other hand, wary of humiliation (as many a working man became), is preoccupied with self-interest. Turning the tables on the male ego in *Tomorrow the World,* Jo enters the quarryman culture, which had been her own father's as a young man, imagining what it would be like for such a macho man as Tom Mulligan to lose his virility, discovering that in a sense there was no way out for working men then:

The party had gone with a swing. They were merry to a man, and now, with the evening drawing to a close, Tom prepared to leave. 'I'd best be off,' he told the hard-drinking quarry-men. 'The missus hasn't been too well, as you know, and even with Nelly watching over her, it's not right to leave her for too long.' He'd had a good night, and now it was time to go.

'Aye, and I'd best be away an' all,' Dave Grundy declared. 'Me own wife's due to birth

any minute. She'd skin me alive if it happened tonight while I were having a bloody good time.'

Laughter greeted his remark, but Ted Louis, a burly fellow with a nasty scar across his lip, had something snide to say. 'We all know about that,' he guffawed, his sly gaze going to Tom, whom he disliked. 'There's not one of us here who ain't fathered a heap o' young 'uns – all except for Tom Mulligan.' His lips curled in a sneer. 'I reckon 'e don't know how to do it right. Happen one of us should show him, eh?'

A terrible silence fell on the party, all eyes on Tom who had turned his face to his tormentor.

Tom Mulligan believes, 'Without pride, a man is nothing!' And, 'with his clothes torn, his face swollen and bloody, one arm hanging limp by his side,' he does manage to salvage his pride, at least in the short-term. But what is the working man's pride becoming? Mulligan refuses his wife the right to question his authority in the home. There is no honour or self-respect in treating a wife the way many of Jo's male characters do. Yet honour and self-respect define pride.

Seeing what he has become leads Tom Mulligan into a moral and emotional cul de sac, and suicide seems the only way out:

Blackburn started out as a small settlement around a bridge over the River Blakewater. As it grew, the town spread to cover the river, and children used to float fires lit on dustbin lids through culverted reaches of it, waiting for the flickering flame to appear when next the river opened out to the sky.

Jo's own memories of childhood were long held in dark reaches of her mind against the pain of enforced exile. Then her imagination lit them up with a fire of its own.

The Sun at the top corner of King Street in Blackburn features strongly in Jo's books, notably in *Alley Urchin*, *Looking Back* and *Cradle of Thorns*, as indeed does the Swan next door.

'Come Friday, the men were worn out, they headed for the pub with the wages. It was a vicious circle,' recalls Jo. 'The Sun was my dad's main haunt... I'd knock on the door and a big navvy would come and say, "Aw, it's Barney's lass, fetch her in." And he'd bring me in and stand me on the counter [pictured here] and I'd sing and dance, and me dad would put his flat cap next to me and they'd all put money into it.'

Thwaites family brewery (pronounced locally without the 'h') was founded in 1797; Dutton's was another of the town's brewers. 'The brewery wagon ambled along across the street, loaded with hefty wooden barrels brimful of draught beer.' *Outcast*.

Jo experienced the compounding effect drink has on poverty, as did the families of many of her friends in the neighbourhood.

'Parkinson Street was home... her comforting world into which she could retreat when things became complicated and painful.' *In Her Father's Sins*, Jo places Queenie's home in Parkinson Street in the Mill Hill area of Blackburn, but she writes of it as Derwent Street, where she herself was born. Jo knew it so well she can tell us that there were 910 cobble stones 'up to Widow Hargreaves at No. 16.'

Above right: Corporation Park is a sanctuary for many of Jo's heroines, among them Eva and Patsy in *Love Me Or Leave Me*, Rosie Selby in *More Than Riches*, and Kelly Wilson in *Somewhere, Someday*, where it is 'so painfully familiar...the place where she had known so much joy.' As for Kelly's brother Michael, so for Jo: 'the only countryside I ever saw were the lawns in Corporation Park.'

1950s smog in Tram Boulevard: 'At a quarter to four the following morning, she was out of bed and watching from the window... Already the ascending curls of smoke were darkening the coming dawn.' *Don't Cry Alone*

'Oh, what a treat it was when she and Auntie Biddy took the walk into town on a market day!' writes Jo in *Her Father's Sins*. The Market Place is central to Jo's memories: in *Don't Cry Alone*, Maisie and Cissie are market flower sellers; in *Alley Urchin*, Molly is taken for a thief; while in *Take This Woman*, Sonny Fareham gives us its sights and sounds – vendors selling their wares, stray dogs scavenging, children bawling, mothers raising their eyes to heaven, and wondering why they ever came out that morning.

'The place was thronging with people, mostly young, mostly screaming on the rides, or strolling arm-in-arm, or pressed up against some stationary object, frantically fumbling each other. The fairground did that to people...'
Looking Back

Jo and her sister Winifred used to work on the hoopla stalls when the fair came to town, but, 'The waltzers were my favourite,' says Jo. 'Still are.'

Pendle Hill, to the northeast of Blackburn, where in the 17th century, 'upon a good-fryday,' there gathered together 'all the most dangerous and wicked and damnable witches in the country, far and near...' Nine of the Pendle witches and their accomplices were hanged.

Eight of those imprisoned came from Samlesbury, a village featured in *The Woman Who Left* and the more recent *Lovers and Liars*, where the love nurtured there between Emily Ramsden and John Hanley is so deep and pure that even their eventual spouses accept it takes priority in the emotional programme of their lives.

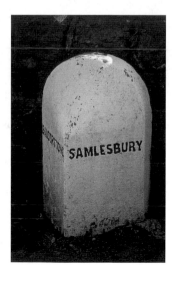

'If you are going to write stories,' says Jo, 'you must live the part of every character.' Time and again it is Jo's women who make the strongest characters. 'The women of Lancashire were a race unto themselves,' she has said. 'They experienced few luxuries, accepting hard work and domineering husbands as part of their unenviable lot.'

Jack stood beside Ted, his curious gaze follow-
ing Ted's stricken stare down into the quarry.
Below was the great bucket, filled with sand
and ready for raising. Above that was the
boom, and hanging from it was Tom Mulligan.
'Oh no!' Jack cried, his face ashen. 'Dear God,
why would he do a thing like that?'

    By the time they cut Tom down, it was too
late.

The hard work, the exhaustion, the frustration, the
humiliation, the indignant rage fired many a Blackburn worker to drink. And many did work hard. 'If
Barty Bendall could lay claim to anything commend-
able,' Jo writes of her father in *Angels Cry Some-*
times, 'it was his great capacity for working hard . . .
no one, family nor drinking partners, could deny
the truth of it. The greatest pity of it all was that
the fruits of his hard labours very rarely served to
assist his family in their times of need, rendered even
needier by his deliberate neglect.'

Drink kept men like Barty, and his real-life
counterpart, in just the kind of spiral of need that
ensured their continued compliance. 'My father's
work was getting him nowhere,' Jo explained, 'he
became a Jekyll and Hyde figure, a wonderful man
and hard-working, until Friday when he would go
to the pub and come home drunk.'

The sadness was that a weakness for drink could

undermine the precious thing that had been won for the working classes in the revolution – what had survived the exploitation – the thing that defined the working-class myth that the mill owners could never get their greedy hands on. The autonomous, independent tradition of the hand-loom weaver had, over 150 years, been ceded to the Industrial Revolution, but this thing had survived, even been strengthened by living in hardship in those closed-in terraces. Jo is specific about what this is in *Don't Cry Alone*, when she writes of Beth Ward: 'Here in Blackburn, with Maisie and her two children, she had found another kind of love, *a deep sense of belonging.*'

The ultimate reality, this working-class sense of belonging to a community – Ruby Miller's 'silver lining' to the cloud of misery that hung over Blackburn in *Nobody's Darling* – is alive in the mainstream novels, not because Jo is milling a good idea, but because she and her characters embody the spirit of a people and evince this sense of belonging, of working-class tradition. Periodically, television soaps and advertisements trade on tradition with a very bastard image. Few draw directly, as Jo does, from the well of experience that makes it true.

'Does that feeling, that "sense of belonging", ever leave you?' I ask.

'No. I read about *Angela's Ashes* and Frank McCourt, who came from Limerick, and the people of Limerick denying it was ever like that. They were

212

ashamed of their roots because they had been poor, they had been hungry, and they wanted to forget it because they had done well and had moved on. I cannot understand that attitude.'

But drink was another compensatory factor for what had happened to her people over two centuries, and those that fell victim to it ensured that they couldn't enjoy this 'belonging' even in their own home. Drink turned the men against the very community to which they belonged. In *Live the Dream*, which opens in 1932, an idyllic marriage is one in which the father doesn't drink. Amy Atkinson's father has 'only ever been the worse for drink once in the whole of his life, and that was when Granddad Atkinson got wed for the second time,' says Amy's mother, Marie. As a result, Amy has strong values of honour and duty. In *Bad Boy Jack*, set in 1895, Robert Sullivan's wife Mathilde leaves the family home with the rent man, after ten years of marriage. Drink precipitates the crisis. Jack and Nancy, their children, used to sit and wait in the dark for their dad to come home, invariably drunk. This is exactly the picture Jo painted of herself and her brother waiting for Barney, her father. The novel deals with the psychological consequences for the children, who blame themselves for where drink leads. 'It wasn't his fault, and it wasn't Mary's fault. It was mine!' says young Jack, who then comes between his father and his subsequent girlfriend, Mary Honeywell.

The 'coming home from the pub' scene that Jo paints in *Looking Back* was typical and remained imprinted on the psyches of the children, in this case Molly Tattersall:

'What's this then, eh?' Frank felt oddly uncomfortable with his eldest daughter's gaze on him. 'What the hell are you staring at,' he said rudely, 'like I've got the pox or summat! And where's yer mam?'

'I'm here, Frank. Leave the lass alone.' Behind him, Amy clung sleepily to the banister.

Taking her roughly by the arm, he dragged her inside. 'So! Yer couldn't even wait up for me, eh, you lazy bitch.'

Instinctively afraid, Amy dropped her gaze, but not Molly. As always, she stood her ground.

'You're drunk,' she said in disgust.

'So what! If I'm drunk it's my money I'm spending, not yourn.' Drawing from Molly's strength, Amy looked up. 'You haven't spent all your wages, have you, Frank?'

'None of your business.' He blundered into a chair and cursed. 'Bloody women!'

'You've not been gambling, have you, Frank?' Amy said fearfully. She knew from old that gambling would take his every penny, and hers too.

He glared at her through bleary eyes. 'And what if I have?'

When he saw her face fall he jeered, 'You'll manage. You always do.'

Suddenly he noticed there was no food on the table. 'Hey! Where's me bloody supper, eh?'

Banging his fist on the table, he screeched like a madman. 'DID YOU HEAR WHAT I SAID, WOMAN? Move your arse and get some food on this table.' His voice fell to a sinister tone. 'Before I do summat I might regret.' Already he was moving towards her.

'Leave her alone, Dad.' Molly took a step forward. 'She's not feeling too good.'

It is no coincidence that Jo's first novel, *Her Father's Sins*, published in 1987, and this one, published thirteen years later, are about the same thing – family dislocation and dysfunction due to drink. It was what Jo's childhood was about and it is to Jo's mum Mary Jane's eternal credit that she had the courage to do something about it.

CHAPTER SIX

Broken Hearts

'Mum used to say that when we were old enough we'd leave,' says Jo. 'Then one day, my dad had gone to work and we were all getting ready for school, but she told us she was leaving my dad. It was quite an awful experience. I cried for weeks. Mum – she was pregnant when she left my dad – she gathered us all together on the Rec, where they used to park the buses overnight. She just drew us all together when Dad had gone to work. She said she was going to her sister's in Dunstable [Bedfordshire] and she wasn't coming back and she was going to take us all with her. There was a lot of crying – "We don't want to go, we want to stay here . . ." She took four of us. Me mam wanted to take us all. It was a terrible time. I was fourteen, not a good time. And my two brothers, Bernard and Richard, who come directly after me, they decided to stay with dad. What a decision to have to make when you are eleven or twelve years old! So that was pretty awful. Not only did I miss my friends and my dad, but my brothers were left behind too. It was so traumatic, leaving them and my dad behind.'

What would the deserted man feel? In *Looking Back* Frank Tattersall's agony is piteous when, with the 'scrawny redhead' he has brought home, he reacts to his wife Amy's letter telling him that she has left him (her leaving takes her into Bedfordshire, as did Jo's mum's). Molly, their daughter, is in attendance:

Just as she had suspected, the minute she had gone, he picked up the letter and began reading it, his jaw dropping in disbelief as he took in the words.

Molly was halfway up the stairs when she heard him yelling, 'Get out of 'ere, you old hag! Get back to the bloody streets where yer belong!'

Pausing, Molly looked down to see her father manhandling the redhead out the front door. When he saw Molly on the stair, he ordered, 'You! Get back down 'ere this minute.'

Taking her time, she returned to the parlour.

Wild-eyed and furious, Frank flung the offending letter across the table. 'What's all this bloody nonsense then? What game does she think she's playing?'

'It's no game.'

Appearing not to have heard, he gave a nervous little laugh. 'Happen she's heard rumours about them streetwomen who keep following me home.' Pacing up and down, he was like a man demented. 'Well, I'll soon put paid to that, 'cos I'm off to the 'orspital right now, and just let the buggers try and throw me out this time!'

'It's no good you going there.' Molly thought it amazing how the shock of that letter seemed to have sobered him up. 'If you read the letter properly, you'll know she's not there.'

'She's bloody there all right, but not for long, 'cos I'm fetching her back 'ere, where she belongs.'

'You're not listening to me, are you?' Molly had expected him to go berserk and turn the place upside down. Instead, it seemed like all the stuffing had been knocked out of him.

Looking at Molly, he cocked his head to one side, his eyes too bright, his voice beginning to crack. 'Aye, that's what I'll do. Yer mam's had time enough now.' Running his hands frantically through his thinning hair, he said, 'No wonder she's writing silly stuff like that. She'll be going out of her mind in that place. Oh, aye. Once our Amy's home, this damned house might get back to normal.'

When he grabbed up his coat from the sofa

218

Molly cried out to him, 'It's no use you going to the Infirmary. She's not there!'

He paused in the doorway, coat in hand, head bowed and his back to her. 'Don't go fooling yourself,' she told him harshly, hating him. 'Mam's gone, thanks to you, and judging by that letter, she's never coming back.'

For what seemed a lifetime, the silence in the little parlour was unbearable.

Frank remained quite still, head hanging low, coat in hand; neither he nor Molly made a move. In the background the clock ticked and from somewhere upstairs came the creaking of a floorboard.

In *Bad Boy Jack*, a much later novel, Jo dissects the emotional response of the father more precisely, after Robert Sullivan is left first by his wife, Mathilde, the mother of his children, and then by his lover, Mary. He is forced to give up his children, and there seems to Robert only one meaningful way out, throwing himself off a railway bridge. Dissuaded, he returns for his children, but they have been despatched to Galloway's Children's Home. The vacuum in Robert's life haunts the reader, and we know he is about to be brought ever lower.

He goes to an inn, shares his sorrow with two apparently sympathetic strangers, Geordie and Marlon, who hatch a plan to rob him. They set upon him on the road outside and leave him with the thought, 'You're not the first bloke to be dumped by a woman, and you'll not be the last.' But there is more to it than that. Robert has had the desire to live taken out of him, and as if Marlon knows it, he sends Robert sprawling under a runaway horse-drawn carriage. Robert is presumed killed.

As in Jo's own thoughts about her parents' split, there are no winners, only losers. The deserted and the escapee come off equally badly. We learn that, 'it filled Mary with shame to desert Robert, [but] she could think of no other way.' She will suffer for doing so. Mary, who has left the family home and made off to Lytham St Anne's on the coast west of Blackburn, is then also dispossessed. While asleep on the train she is relieved by a common thief of her tapestry bag, which contains everything she owns. Readers of Jo's earlier novel, *Miss You Forever*, cannot fail to link Mary to the vagrant Kathleen Peterson, whose whole life is also contained in a tapestry bag, and who finds her way to Lytham, too, before coming to a horrible end. Kathleen came to Jo after a friend told her about an old lady who had been found beaten up on the streets of London. 'She'd been taken to hospital and died. And when they put an ad in the papers and put out announcements on the radio – the Authorities tried to trace her family or anyone who knew her – nobody came forward and they had to put her in a pauper's grave. That really upset me; how can an old lady who had gone all through life not have any friends, or even enemies to spit on her grave? The thread of that character has come through a couple of books because she affected me so deeply,' Jo explains.

Then, of course, there are the children. For the children caught in the middle there are equally hopeless expectations. Robert's two, Jack and Nancy, are separated (as Jo's brothers and sisters were) and sent to different homes with adopted parents.

In *Looking Back*, when Amy Tattersall leaves the family home, she leaves her children because her boyfriend Jack will not take them on. She is, naturally, deeply troubled about what she is doing, and we can surely read Jo's mother's anguish in this, for she left some of her children behind:

> *In her mind's eye she could see little Eddie, running round the parlour, his napkin round his ankles; and Bertha, laughing, always laughing. Then there was Milly and Georgie – and Molly. Oh Molly, what have I done to you?*
>
> *But in spite of her sorrow, she could never go back. Not now she had found the courage to leave.*

She writes her eldest, Molly, a letter:

Dearest Molly,
I know what I'm doing is wrong, and I hope
there will come a day when you will find it in
your heart to forgive me.

For too many years, I've been your father's
dogsbody. Not a day has gone by when he
hasn't proved how little he cares for me. I'm a
convenience to him, and that's all I'll ever be.
It's too late for him to change now, and besides,
somewhere along the way I've changed. I'm not
the young girl he wed. I'm a woman, with a
woman's feelings. I've got a right to some
respect and consideration. I've borne his
children and taken his abuse, and now the only
feelings I have for him are anger and disgust.

When Jo's mother left home and took her and her
sisters with her out of Blackburn, Jo lost her brothers
and she lost her father, and however difficult he may
have been at times, Jo never fell out of love with
Barney. That loss could never be put right. Laura
Blake's regret and sadness at the loss of her father
is almost tangible in *Take This Woman*, as is Beth
Ward's in *Don't Cry Alone*. Beth sees where her
father is wrong, but knows that he is a victim of his
own misguided perception of life and incapable of
doing other than he does. Here she looks down at
his lifeless body, but the loss she feels has nothing to
do with his death:

In that moment before she turned away, Beth glanced lovingly at her father's still body. His eyes were closed, but she could still see the unforgiving look in them – the terrible accusation. The pain was gone from his face, but it was not gone from her heart. She loved him. Nothing would ever change that. She had lost him. But Death had not taken him from her. No. It was nothing so simple as Death that had parted them.

Beth feels to blame, and the question of blame is again an issue in the more recent *Live the Dream*. Roy, whose father was killed in a fight in prison after a robbery that went wrong, when Roy was twelve is advised by his girlfriend, Daisy: 'You have to believe that what happened was not your fault. I know what it's like for parents to do bad things that frighten you, and sometimes you get the blame. It makes it difficult to think you can rely on people . . .' Later there's more advice from Daisy, which comes from the heart: 'You mustn't feel sorry for yourself, and you mustn't think you're the only one who's ashamed of their parents.' Then she confesses that her own parents 'fight and squabble all the time . . . they hurt each other until they draw blood.' Airing the problems they have both experienced with their parents makes Roy feel, '"You and me were made for each other." Now that the air was cleared and they understood each other, they went off down the street hand in hand, making plans together – and beginning to fall in love.'

Just as Beth feels to blame and sees the unforgiving look in her dead father's eyes, so Roy feels the kind of guilt many a child has felt when their parents fought. Thinking about blame, I say to Jo that I had noticed that her more recent novels seem less hard on the father figure, and even in the character of Barty Bendall, in *Angels Cry Sometimes*, there is a suggestion that maybe Marcia, his wife, was partly to blame for what happened between them. When Barty dies, Marcia's sense of loss, and perhaps guilt, spills over onto the page, a lament to the paradox of love and bitterness that characterised an era. She seems at least partly to absolve him of blame:

As she looked down at the prematurely aged face of Barty Bendall, Marcia reproached herself. The wicked features had relaxed in that quiet moment before his life and his torment were over. 'I'm sorry, Barty,' she murmured, the tears spilling down her face. 'Oh I'm so sorry!'

'It seems she tried so hard to hate him . . . but she found herself pitying him. Had she, in reality, been to blame in some way?' I said to Jo, who is as fiercely protective of her privacy as Amy Atkinson in *Live the Dream*, when talk turns to her father.

'Six of one, half a dozen of the other,' Jo replied. 'I look back and I think that the bad times were usually weekends, after me dad had had his wages and gone to the pub. He was not a bad man at all, he was a good man, he had a wonderful sense of humour . . .' She paused for a moment, before recalling her father especially warmly. 'He was a good man, but he was not demonstrative. That was the thing. He didn't display his feelings towards his children. But towards my sister Winifred he was very, very warm. Not so warm towards me. And all my childhood I can remember thinking, wouldn't it be nice if my dad would put his arms round me and say, "I love you." But he never did.'

Oh, the complexities of the father–daughter relationship, and how especially difficult when part of the character of the northern working-class man was not to be emotionally demonstrative. That is a loss never to be restored. I recalled William Woodruff's story of his father giving a bunch of flowers to his wife, awkwardly, almost abruptly handing them to her, a muffled grunt saying all that could be said.

Barney will have found it doubly difficult to express his feelings for his daughter, who sided so dramatically with her mother. Was that the 'unforgiving look' in Beth's father's eyes? And then Jo brought into the house this story-telling talent, quite foreign to him – 'the last thing he wanted to hear was any of my airy-fairy nonsense,' Jo said. 'As far back as I can remember I always had that feeling that there was something better than Derwent Street or Henry Street, and that if you worked hard enough you would get there.'

'Maybe he saw and mistrusted that, saw it as a criticism of his way of life,' I said.

'Dad never listened when I told him I wanted to be a writer,' she replied. 'But Mam would always encourage me to do what I wanted.'

The loss Jo felt clearly went beyond the geographical distance that her mother had put between her and her father. It cannot escape dedicated readers of Jo's novels that the orphaning of her heroines is a recurring theme, and in particular most of them are touched by the loss of the father figure. Yet, when, five years ago in a telephone conversation with Jo, I suggested that the loss of her father seems to be the source of her inspiration, she was actually taken aback. 'You know, it is so strange that you say that, because I haven't consciously done that. Though the book that I am working on now [*The Woman Who Left*] . . . you saying that . . . my God! I have done it again in this book! I never realised I had done that. You are right. How strange.'

The loss of her father is not something of which Jo can let go, any more than Kelly can in *Somewhere, Someday*:

'*Some time back there were an old fella lived along the canal. He had this gangrenous leg, d'yer see? Finally, the doctors gave him a choice. "Have the leg cut off, or lose yer life," that's what they told him. He let them cut off his leg, an' d'yer know, the old bugger lived to be eighty-six year old.*'

Kelly saw what Charlie was getting at. 'You're saying, what happened to my father – everything – that it's like that man's leg, filling me with poison and destroying my life?' It seemed so simple, and yet it wasn't.

'*Aye, lass, that's what I'm saying. You've carried that burden long enough, and now yer have to cut it out of yer life and give yerself a chance to recover.*'

Happiness is always just around the corner in Jo's stories, as if there hangs a veil between 'what is' and 'what might have been'. So it was for countless families in Blackburn between about 1830 and 1950, whatever the nature of their loss. The novels have helped Jo resolve hers, but should anyone doubt what it has taken to bring her this far, they should remember that the alienation of father and daughter came at fourteen, a sensitive time – and listen to Kitty Marsh in *Living a Lie*:

227

In her dreams she was suffocating, lost in a swirl of dark fog, her lungs hot and burning. Asleep, she fought against it. She opened her eyes but couldn't see. 'DADDY!' The fog tasted sour, forcing itself into her mouth, her body. While her senses weakened, her desperate screams grew louder: 'DADDY, HELP ME!'

Suddenly he was there. 'Don't be afraid,' he told her softly. 'Hold on to me.' Echoes of her mother's voice haunted her. 'You mustn't run away . . . keep hold of my hand.' She was afraid he meant to hurt her too, but she couldn't fight him, she couldn't breathe. 'Please don't kill me, Daddy!' Her eyes closed and she was at his mercy.

So deep ran Jo's own feelings that a series of novels, kept separate from her main output, insisted themselves upon her. 'A very strange thing has arisen out of my relationship with my father. I never intended writing frightening books,' she told me. 'But some years ago I suddenly started writing under my mother's name [Jane Brindle] and these books are very, very sinister, psychological thrillers. They're dark, sinister books which I never meant to write, but they creep up behind me and push me so hard that eventually I just have to do it. I think those feelings come from my childhood when I was afraid

228

and hungry and emotions ran high between Mam and Dad.'

What is so interesting about this development is its spontaneity. The books came to Jo unbidden. They insisted themselves upon her. They are all the more telling on account of this, because they are her unconscious speaking. The terrifying burden of the first of the series, *Scarlet*, makes this point at the outset, choosing for its location the cellar of the Pengallys' house on the edge of Exmoor in North Devon.

We already know that the cellar was a significant element of Jo's childhood experience. There are cellar scenes throughout the early stories, based on the cellar in the Brindles' house in Henry Street. 'A great big cellar,' Jo recalls, 'it was quite scary, that one. I remember seeing rats running around our feet in the toilet and water running into the cellar.' In the novels, however, the cellar is a place of terror, connected not with rats, but with the violence of a father returning home from the pub the worse for drink, as it is for little Kelly in *Somewhere, Someday*:

> *My mam told my brother Michael that when it got really bad, he was to take me down to the coal cellar – you couldn't hear anything down there. We'd huddle together in the dark and he'd tell me stories of little people with wings and pointed feet, and how they lived in the cellar and hid whenever we went down.' She*

smiled. 'He said that if you believed in them, they would grant a wish. I believed it all, and wished to go away and never come back.' The quiet smile melted beneath the sadness. 'But the beating went on, and I stopped believing.'

In *Scarlet*, however, we are a step away from conscious reality – the cellar no longer feels like a real place, we are entering the cellar of Jo's unconscious mind. It comes to represent Scarlet's personal unconscious, and harbours a deep, dark secret too terrible to tell.

'Thank God you found me, Vincent.' Hannah Pengally was lying at the foot of the cellar steps, one leg bent at a peculiar angle, her pretty face contorted with pain and her blue eyes moist with tears. 'I was on my way down to fill the coal bucket . . .'

Hannah is having a baby – twins to be precise – although Hannah doesn't know it, nor will she know it, because she passes out while the delivery is undertaken by her blacksmith husband Vincent in the cellar.

The first child to be born is Scarlet, 'dark-haired like her father and perfect in every detail'. The second is a boy, horribly deformed. Vincent, repulsed, leaves it, wraps his daughter against the cold damp atmosphere of the cellar and then remembers that three-year-old Silas, whose mother had warned Vincent on her death bed that he would be cursed if he did not look after him, has witnessed the whole gory business from a dark corner.

Scarlet and Hannah are taken into the house. Silas is left in the cellar with the deformed baby. Three days pass before Vincent returns to find only Silas, no baby. There is the thought that Silas, a primitive, Heathcliff-style ragged boy of Exmoor, has somehow disposed of the creature.

Vincent is violent, cruel and a harsh disciplinarian to everyone, including his wife. Scarlet grows up beautiful and brave, deriving no small amount of strength from her friendship with Silas, which is strictly forbidden by Vincent and occasions many an attempt by him to subdue Silas and break Scarlet's spirit. Silas, who has grown up handsome and with a fine physique, sleeps not in the house, but in a barn, and is regularly beaten, and once even branded, by Vincent.

Hannah recalls nothing of the birth, or her deformed son, but has a worrying sense that something is being concealed from her or has somehow eluded her conscious mind. The child, of course, did not die, and as the threat is delivered as to what will happen when this wild, deformed creature is on the loose on the moor, the stage is set for a suspense thriller in the tradition of *The Hound of the*

Baskervilles, itself set on Exmoor and written by Arthur Conan Doyle, whose first novel was *A Study in Scarlet* (1887).

Central to this novel, however, is what Jo refers to as Scarlet's 'unique and destructive relationship that had evolved between her and her father.' Vincent loves her in the only way he can love. He idolises her and is violently set against any man taking her innocence, while at the same time lasciviously enjoying her budding beauty himself. It is an unhealthy closeness they share. 'Even as a child she was always terrified that he knew exactly what she was thinking.' She fears him, and there is a sexual tension and suggestion of abuse: at issue is Scarlet's refusal 'to submit. She would not gratify him, never again, in any way!'

It emerges that Scarlet's un-named brother is being looked after by an old herbalist in the woods. The boy is classed as savage, a monster who doesn't know what love is and can only hate. But the herbalist is dedicated to him (fatally, as it turns out).

Meanwhile, Vincent stands custodian of the cellar, allowing nobody in, just as the father stands custodian of the secret fears lurking in the author's unconscious.

Scarlet herself had been allowed in the cellar only once, and that was many years ago, when her father had given in to her persistent requests to 'show me where I was born'. The dark stain was still there. And so was the evil atmosphere that had marked the event. Scarlet had sensed something in that cellar, something that had created discord deep inside her.

Then one day, on Vincent's death bed, her fears are realised.

Her eyes washed over the body, still a bulk of a man, pushing up from beneath the clothes, his chest rising and falling with that painful rasping breathing . . . relieved, quietly smiling . . . she dared to move nearer, peering into that strange face and hoping the breathing would stop. Willing it to stop. How easy it would be, she thought, how effortlessly she could trap that irritating, broken sound with the tips of her fingers, trap it in his throat, press her fingers into the grey parchment and squeeze – squeeze until the sound was no more . . . The long thick fingers twitched erratically. He was disturbed. Scarlet knew it was her thoughts that had disturbed him. Even as a child she was always terrified that he knew exactly what she was thinking. The fear flooded back. Quickly! Get away! BUT IT WAS TOO LATE. In a swift snake-like movement that almost stopped her heart, his fingers leapt out and locked around her wrist. The cold grey eyes flicked open, piercing her like hard glinting steel, 'I knew you'd come back.' . . . His fingers dug into her flesh, tugging her down to him. She could feel the acrid stench of his breath on her face. His mouth opened to kiss her.

Suddenly she was screaming. Writhing to free herself, with her free hand striking him again and again until the skin on his forehead burst open in a shower of crimson spots. Still he clung to her, his long jagged nails snapping as they sliced deep into her flesh. Then, suddenly weakened by her onslaught, he relaxed his grip, and Scarlet ran.

She kept on running, her mind a whirl of confusion. Got to get away! Her heart skipped a beat. She was being pursued! He was out of bed. Following her! She began running down the stairs two at a time. In her frantic haste she slipped, her ankle doubled up beneath her, the pain shooting through her body like knives. GET UP! GET UP! From the corner of her eye she saw the dark shadow looming above her. Quickly! There was no time to make it to the front door. She must hide. HIDE! But where? She was a child again, playing hide and seek and her mammy could never find her. The kitchen. Dear God, help me. Limping badly, with the pain dimming her senses, she found her way to the kitchen and into the old shaft where the disused dumb waiter stood. Silently closing the hatch behind her, she curled up in a ball, afterwards remaining perfectly still and hardly daring to breathe. In the distance she could hear the approaching footsteps muffled and terrifying. When they came closer and filled her with such fear that the sweat trickled down her face, she held her breath, her big black eyes turned towards the shaft door, expecting any minute to see it flung open.

The scene provoked letters from readers disturbed by the intensity of Scarlet's fears. They had no reason to know that that intensity emanates from the fact that Scarlet's nightmare is a reliving of a real-life experience of her creator. 'Scarlet is hiding in the dumb waiter,' Jo told me. 'She is absolutely petrified because she can hear her father's feet coming down the stairs, and she knows she is going to get a real good hiding, so she is hiding in there. That was me. It happened in the house in Henry Street in Blackburn. A lady wrote to me and said she had read this scene and her heart was beating ten to the dozen because she was so frightened it was me in that dumb waiter!'

CHAPTER SEVEN

Leaving Home

Jo's mum showed her mettle in 1955. 'When I look back,' Jo says, 'I think how hard it was, to go two hundred miles away and not know where we were going to end up.' There was a plan, on leaving Blackburn, to make for Mary's sister – the real Auntie Biddy – in Dunstable, Bedfordshire, but, like Nell Reece in *Cradle of Thorns*, the fleeing group stayed awhile in Ridgmont, a beautiful little village ten miles or so south of Bedford and close to Woburn.

Cradle of Thorns is set in 1890. Seventeen-year-old Nell – pretty, strong-spirited and with a mind of her own – is three months pregnant after a one-time liaison with her employer, Lord of the Manor Vincent Morgan. The impending birth and the cruelty of Aunt Lilian impels Nell from the family home, close to Blackburn, to wander about the countryside in precisely the area to which Jo, her siblings and mother were drawn sixty years later. Like Nell in the novel, Jo's mum was pregnant, which can't

236

have made her flight any easier. She would need all her natural self-sufficiency and strength, together with the Christian values rewarded in the novel, to survive.

Jo has picked a classic literary vehicle to portray the most traumatic incident of her life to date. Besides the constant references to her mother's flight from Blackburn in 1955, the narrative finds significant echoes in Charles Dickens's novel, *The Old Curiosity Shop*, in particular Little Nell Trent's flight and wandering about the country with her grandfather. Even Little Nell's friendship with the honest lad, Kit Nubbles, is recalled by Jo in Nell Reece's friendship with the 'cheeky little Cockney lad', also called Kit, who makes her the cradle of thorns for her baby daughter, when finally she is born.

The death of Little Nell was, in its day, one of the most celebrated scenes in fiction, and is recalled in the emotive scene in *Cradle of Thorns* when Kit emplores Nell to 'get better; I ain't got nobody but you'. In Jo's novel, Nell doesn't die because she has her daughter to live for, just as Mary Brindle didn't succumb during her flight because she had Jo, her siblings and the unborn Alec to live for.

This is the message of the novel, which is alive with maternal values and Christian symbolism, especially Catholic values, with their emphasis on mothering and the sacred nature of the Mother of Christ. Aside from the obvious Christian parallel of the cradle of thorns with Christ's crown of thorns as a symbol of suffering, Nell comes upon her own mother confined in a convent in Woburn dedicated to Mary Magdalene, who is the woman Christ cured of evil spirits and is usually taken to have been a prostitute. Then, when Nell starts to give birth she is despatched to Miss Dawson's Home for Gentlewomen, which turns out to be a brothel. Lottie, a prostitute, helps her; and Nell finds out the good in her, describing her as an angel. But the values that win out are Nell's values, which are, above all, maternal. Jo's identification of Nell with her mother, whose name is Mary, which is also the name of the mother of Christ, reminds us that this is a novel celebrating her mother's courage in taking her children away from the violence of home. Those who turn Nell away, beware! Those who, like Vincent, the father of Nell's child, declare, 'The mother is of no consequence', will not prosper.

After a rough night in Bedford town, Nell had travelled about four miles [south] along the main road before cutting off to narrower lanes which would take her into the farming community. At every stop along the way she had tried for work and been turned away. It was a heart-destroying experience.

Mid-morning now, rambling along the lanes and singing softly to herself, Nell did not give up hope. Instead, she kept her eyes open and

stayed alert ... 'There must be work here-
abouts,' she muttered, her blue eyes scanning
the fields. 'And I'm not ready for the knacker's
yard yet.'

These narrow country lanes are still evident, although today there is, all the while, the background
buzz of traffic from the M1, which smashed through
the area some years after the Brindles made it their
own. Here is the cluster of little villages that Jo has
used as settings for various novels. Woburn Sands,
where she herself lives today, features in *Born to
Serve* – Mr Marshall's big Tudor house, Tall Gables,
is to be found in the village. Nearby Salford is the
setting of Jo's recent novel *The Journey*. While Hill-
tops, the farm and home of the Sullivan family in
Bad Boy Jack, which Jo writes is thirty minutes away
from Bedford, is located in neighbouring Halcutt:
'The farm is tucked right away; you can't see it from
the road,' says Jo.

Readers of *Cradle of Thorns* will know that as
Nell approaches the area along the Ampthill Road,
she meets John Butler, who is being pursued by
bailiffs. In desperation, Butler fires his farm cottage
and loads his cart with goods, urging Nell to drive
it to 'a hamlet called Ridgmont [and] find a man
by the name of Albert Slater. He'll take the goods
from you and you can be on your way ... Whatever
happens, *don't turn back.*'

In Ridgmont, the man she believes to be Albert Slater turns out to be his brother and his murderer, Albert's body having been consigned, appropriately enough in the context of Jo's fiction, to a cellar. 'Where the brother was murdered and was left in the cellar ... that house really is in Ridgmont,' Jo told me.

The journey to Ridgmont was painstakingly slow. There were few signs along the narrow, meandering lanes, and Nell had to stop and ask the way several times.

At last, just as the sun was beginning to lose its glory, she came into Ridgmont hamlet by way of the Ampthill Road. 'My! This is a lovely place,' she remarked, looking from one side of the street to the other. The old square church with its pretty tower stood to the left of her, and to the right was an ancient inn with black-timbered gables and flower-filled gardens. Both sides of the street were lined with quaint cottages. Children played outside. There were bairns in prams and mothers chatting, and a lazy, easy feeling to the place that immediately put Nell at ease.

Today, it is impossible to turn a blind eye to the monstrous juggernauts that find their way through the village on their way to the motorway, and so absurd do they look edging their way around the tight corners that it beggars belief that they be allowed to crash through such beauty as can be found here, just off Junction 13 of the M1. The houses, church and pretty gardens are as Jo describes, and the patterned brickwork and inset timbers of the best of the houses makes for stunning architecture. When Jo and her family arrived here in the mid-1950s, out of grimy Blackburn, she must have thought she had landed in Paradise.

'The motorway wasn't there when I arrived, of course. It did take away a lot of character from the village,' she admits sadly. 'It seemed like the middle of nowhere when we arrived, though the brickworks were there.'

I realise that is why the houses are so stunningly crafted out of brick, of course – all are products of the famous local brickworks. 'You know, where all those industrial units are, that was the brickworks,' Jo told me, and everything fell into place.

My mind immediately turned to the passage in *Angels Cry Sometimes*, where Curt Ratheter, Marcia's estranged first husband, stands 'steeped in thought, his face a serious study as he looked first one way and then the other. The road to the right would take him far south to the Bedfordshire brickworks and a new life. To the left was Blackburn, where thanks to Nantie Bett, he knew Marcia and his two daughters to be living. Straight on would take him along the road to Accrington and to Fran Ratheter. After long agonising moments, when his every instinct beckoned him towards Blackburn and the woman whose image had kept him sane these past lonely years, Curt stood up tall, thrust his hands into his pockets and, with a sigh which reached every corner of his being, turned right.'

Here, as it happens, Jo's mum also met her old flame and took up with him: 'Everyone who lived in the surrounding village worked in the brickworks,' explained Jo, 'unless they were farmers, and that is where every man worked who lived on the estate at the top of the hill where we lodged.'

This was the Brogborough estate. 'Brogborough was where I grew and flourished,' remembers Jo, 'and it's where every member of every household was family.' Nearly fifty years later she was invited back by the families on the estate to 'open' a meadow which was to be turned over to the people of the area.

'They were all tied houses, tied to the brickworks. Marston Valley owned them,' said Jo. 'Like the tied cotton mills in Blackburn. You couldn't live in one of those houses unless you worked at the brickworks, and a lot of the women worked there, too, in the canteens, painting the bricks inside the sheds before they went into the kilns to be cooked – not the women, the bricks!

'It was like a community. Because every house on

that hill, all the men and most of the women, worked together. So, the community spirit was strong and taken from where they lived to where they worked. Everyone knew everyone else. It was like a huge family.'

There is an unbelievably romantic story attached to Jo's coming to Ridgmont. One day – 'it was about four o'clock in the afternoon' – she met someone who was to change her life completely. 'This tall, blond man came striding across the road,' Jo recalls. 'I was over at the working men's club with a few girls and we were just messing around, and I looked up the street and I saw this tall, slim, blond-haired boy walking across and I couldn't take my eyes off him. That was it! I was in love!'

Jo was fifteen, and her future husband, Ken Cox, the tall, blond man walking across the road, was nineteen. They married the following year and had two sons, Spencer and Wayne, now thirty-three and thirty-one. They were married for forty-four years, until Ken died a few years ago.

Immediately, Ken proved himself a caring adjunct to Jo's family. 'He took us all under his wing. We actually got lodgings with his parents. They say there's no such thing as love at first sight, but I knew Ken was the man for me as soon as I laid eyes on him. Unfortunately he didn't feel the same. He thought I was too young for him. But I was smitten; he was so smart . . . I would be following him everywhere and

I was so young. I used to hang around waiting for him all the time, but he would say, "Go away, you're just a snotty-nosed kid." Then we just became friends. I was friends with his sister, Marion, and we'd just start chatting, you know? Then after a while I wore him down, and bit by bit he fell in love with me. Whether he actually fell in love with me when he turned round and looked at me that day I don't know, but he was very, very special.

'Then we went to my Auntie Biddy's in Dunstable. My Uncle Fred, that's Auntie Biddy's husband, worked in the rubber factory there, and Auntie Biddy, who was a very stern lady, very disciplined, quite frightening to me and yet she had a heart of gold, she insisted that as I had left school at fourteen, I should go and work in the rubber factory. However, Uncle Fred thought it was absolutely not on the cards for me to work at the rubber factory – not the place for a young girl – and there was quite an argument. But Auntie Biddy was adamant, I was to go and work in that rubber factory. Mum had gone into hospital to have the baby, and I ran away and found my way back to Ken. I ran away to his mum. I walked all the way from Dunstable back to Ridgmont!'

This is a distance of some ten miles, Ridgmont being about midway between Bedford to the north and Dunstable to the south. Jo making such an 'escape' on foot is an indication not only of her feelings for Ken, but also of the trauma she was going through. Leaving Blackburn for the south, however unexpectedly promising in some respects, had been a terrible wrench. 'It was an incredibly traumatic time,' Jo admits. 'Although my family had always been loud and chaotic, we were all very close. It was terrible being divided up like that. I suddenly felt displaced . . .' Her first feelings will have been Kelly's on her exile from the town in *Somewhere, Someday*:

> *Collecting her feelings, she paused. 'I began thinking about Blackburn and everything, and it was as though I'd left something behind.' She gave a small bitter laugh. 'It's hard to explain, but it was my life.' Angry tears filled her eyes. 'And they took it away.'*

And things only got worse. 'We ended up moving from lodgings to lodgings, which made me feel very insecure. I had to change school every six months and, to make it worse, this chap Mam had taken up with was a real bully and used to make comments that would belittle her and destroy her confidence. She used to cry a lot, and although I hated the fact that she stayed with him, I knew she did so to give us some stability.'

Living this way made Jo feel her life was spiralling out of control, 'that there's nothing you can do to make things better,' as she put it. 'It's a horrible feeling, and I longed for some security. Above all else, I wanted to feel that I could influence my own destiny.'

Ken became her anchor, so much so that only two years after leaving Blackburn, she felt bold enough to return to her homeland with him, 'to meet me dad and me brothers and that'.

The trip did not go well. 'Me dad was a little bit hostile towards him, he wasn't warm like he normally was. Maybe because I was only sixteen and he knew that Ken was the one ... a father's protective instincts. Then, later, when I wrote to him and told him that Ken and I were getting married, and I would be so proud for him to come and give me away, he wrote, "I am not giving you away. You are too young. I will not be there." My father refused to come to my wedding. He thought I was too young to get married. He refused to come and give me away. That really did upset me. He should have been by my side. Instead of that, it was a relative of Ken's. My father wouldn't even give his permission, my mother did, my mam gave her blessing ... but that broke my heart, the fact that he wouldn't come down and give me away. We were married on Easter Saturday 1958. I was sixteen and Ken was nineteen.' It was, in fact, three months before Jo's seventeenth birthday.

From that moment on, impressively, Jo did take

control of her life. When the boys started school, she studied for the O- and A-level exams that had eluded her in Blackburn, while at the same time working in a factory making belts for plastic macs. 'I did this because I felt as if I had missed out on the learning and the excitement of achieving things. I went for three years to evening classes after working in a plastics factory all day. It felt wonderful; I'd asked for extra assignments. I did very well and got A-levels in Sociology, English and History, with A grades and distinctions, though I found the O-level maths lessons very hard because I had in mind that frightening maths teacher at school in Blackburn! I'd already applied for teacher-training at Bletchley College, got my teaching cert., and then I was offered a place at Lucy Cavendish College, Cambridge.'

Lucy Cavendish is the only college of Cambridge University to offer (exclusively) mature women returnees the opportunity to pursue a higher education that they may have deferred or interrupted. Acceptance was a quite extraordinary achievement – from dodging lessons in Blackburn's Corporation Park to being offered a place as an undergraduate at the most prestigious university in Britain. However, in true, pragmatic style, Jo turned the offer down. Going to Cambridge would have meant living on site and splitting up the family. There was nothing more likely to concentrate Jo's mind than a threat to family.

'I was offered a place at Lucy Cavendish, but you had to live in and I said I can't do that. It was an echo of my mam and my dad, of my family splitting up. I could not leave my family for two or three years.' Instead she went to teacher-training college locally and began teaching English and History at a local Comprehensive school. 'I taught for fifteen years and loved every minute. After the kids left the school they were still knocking on my door to say hello. It was just great.'

Then, in the 1970s, Ken's haulage business, secured against the house they now owned, succumbed to the recession, and Jo and Ken lost their home. In *Living a Lie*, Jenkins' Haulage is clearly Ken's company. In the novel things have not been going well, and now Michael Norden, who owns a string of garages around the country, and with whom Harry has the principal haulage contract, phones to tell him he is not renewing it. Knocked sideways, Harry, who has just come in from the rain, tries to inject some humour into the exchange:

'You can't tell me you're getting some other haulier to do it cheaper than I do? Christ! If I did it any cheaper, I'd have to pedal the stuff about.'

'Sorry, mate. I've no more work for you.'

'Are you having me on?' It seemed inconceivable that this contract should be ended. He had

never once let this man down, and always kept his rates trimmed to the bone to accommodate him.

'I've decided not to renew the contract.'

'And that's it?' Harry couldn't believe his ears. 'Can we sit round the table and discuss it?'

'Sorry, mate. I won't be renewing your contract and that's an end to it.' The phone was replaced and Harry was left looking into the receiver. 'What the hell's going on?' Carefully replacing the receiver he went to the filing cabinet and took out a batch of papers. Spreading them on the desk, he glanced through them. 'There's something very strange about all this,' he muttered. 'That's the third contract I've lost in as many weeks.'

Taking a towel from the cupboard, he rubbed his hair dry and poured out a measure of brandy. He needed to think rationally about this business, and for the minute he was both angry and confused. 'Calm down, Jenkins,' he told himself. 'Don't go jumping to any conclusions. There has to be an explanation.'

After a while he began to thaw. He worked on his ledger and balanced his books ready for the accountant, and even there he could see how drastically his orders had dropped. Another thing was the silence. Lately, the

*phone didn't ring either. 'It's like I've got the
bloody plague!'*

Jo and Ken went back to live with Ken's parents, but
one son had to move in with other relatives owing
to lack of space, and this would have been less than
a happy arrangement for Jo, who had so deliberately
avoided seeing her family split up for the second time
when offered the place at Cambridge.

With the family threatened, she again took control
and showed her amazing energy. 'We lost everything.
We had nothing again, but we picked ourselves up,
dusted ourselves down, and got on with it. We had
to beg the council to give us a house,' she recalls.
'All they could offer was an unbelievably filthy, semi-
derelict house. There was graffiti on the walls, people
had broken in, windows were missing, the roof had
caved in and anything of value had been ripped out.
We ran from this place, but the Authorities said
if we didn't take this we wouldn't get any house. So
we rolled up our sleeves and renovated it from top
to bottom. The neighbours were using the garden as
a tip – we must have taken out about six skip-loads
of rubbish when we first moved in. It took a long
time to get the place right, but in the end we grew
to love it. We lived there for seventeen years.'

More hardship and loss were to pass before publication of her first novel, *Her Father's Sins*. 'In those
years a succession of things happened to us,' Jo

recalls. 'We both lost our parents, then I lost a young brother. For two years our bad luck just went on and on ... I came out the other end realising you have to be grateful for what you have – and that if you want anything, you must go out and get it. You either go down and stay down, or you get up and fight back. It was a really rough time.'

It was quite a fight. Jo's health suffered, and it was while she was in hospital that she made the big break. 'The whole time I was teaching, I had wanted to write. It was always at the back of my mind, but I hadn't had time. And then it was as if life suddenly said, "Stop, before you fall down." I was confined to bed and I was going stir crazy, when a visiting teaching colleague said, "Why don't you write that book you're always on about?" So I did, and I put it in a drawer, and then about two years later Ken said, "Why did you write that book?" And I said, "Because I wanted the world to know what it was like." He said, "They're not going to know if it's in the drawer." So, I sent it away and it was accepted straight away. They wanted anything else I'd written in two years, which was three more books, and I've written two a year ever since.' And, she might have added, sold fifteen million copies of them worldwide.

'I wrote stories about the people I grew up with. Once I started, the words just flowed off the pages. I'd be writing when the nurse came to switch off the light, then I'd switch it back on again and carry on writing. I wrote the first book in six weeks – *Her Father's Sins*. It was a bestseller in 1987, it really was an overnight bestseller,' she recalls, with as much delight as when first she was informed.

'The same year the publishers accepted it, Ken and the two boys entered me into a *Mirror* Group "Superwoman of Britain" competition right across the nation to find someone who had come through to do well against all obstacles. I think there were four thousand contestants. I knew nothing about it until one day I picked up the phone and someone said, "Josephine Cox, please. I'd like to interview her."

'I said, "What for? Who are you?" And she said she had to interview me. I had eight interviews. They had four thousand entries and they whittled it down to twelve and the twelve went off to the Dorchester Hotel. Then Derek Nimmo and a whole panel of people interviewed us one after another. Three or four days – absolutely out of this world! Then we were all told to line up in the Savoy Hotel. Third, second . . . and then they called out my name. I couldn't believe it! I won £1000 and a silver rose bowl. What a way to launch the book!'

Jo had first put pen to paper in 1984, just a year after Cicely Bridge Cotton Mill, where her mother had worked her fingers to the bone in the carding room, was closed down. I asked her whether Mary had ever returned to the town.

'Yes, she did, but not until after my dad died. I don't recall her going up there for a long, long time. Oh, how I remember her at Cicely Bridge Mill. Do you know, I watched it being knocked down? Ken and I went up there. I showed him where me mam worked and where I pushed the little babbies in the pram to meet her when I was about nine. We got about halfway up and there was this cordon across the road and all these cranes and things. I got out and had a look and it was half-demolished. I couldn't believe they were taking it down . . . I stood and cried. Did you read *Let Loose the Tigers*, when they were pulling this street down and Queenie cried, not because they were knocking a street down but because they were knocking her history down? Where flesh and blood had lived and breathed and slept and worked, and it was going and it would be no more. That – the way she felt – is exactly how I felt that day when I saw them knock down Cicely Bridge Mill.'

It was the end of an era. But even on her first trip back with Ken in the 1950s Jo had witnessed great change, and would now write about it, returning in every one of those early novels to the land of her birth, and recording her first visit in the mid-Fifties in *Somewhere, Someday*:

Nothing had changed. And yet it had changed. Seeing it all again was like standing outside a mirror looking in. The image was familiar, and yet somehow it was a stranger looking back. As though she was not part of it all, and never had been.

It was a weird, unnerving, yet exhilarating experience.

By 1957 there had been a two-thirds reduction of employment in the cotton industry. By 1965 the job tally was almost halved again. In 1972 there were only 6572 jobs left, and by 1981 this had decreased to 3404. Just two years later there were only five Blackburn mills left in operation. There had been efforts to revitalise the economy of the area by diversifying into engineering. In twenty years from 1931, the number of engineering jobs had doubled, and expansion has continued in recent years. In modern times, too, the town has seen other major initiatives, such as the canal waterway scheme in conjunction with local business. And in 2003 they were able to report a drop in the number of unemployed claiming benefit to 2.4%, which is on a par with the rate for England and Wales and is a long way from being the highest claimant count of the areas considered only twenty-two months earlier.

In the Fifties and for a decade or more following, however, Jo would have witnessed the bleakest of pictures. Nothing, it seemed, could take up the slack left by cotton, and whatever was achieved by new industries the overall picture was gloom. Job losses continued, and Blackburn frequently had four or five per cent more unemployed than some of the bleakest-hit areas in the North.

In an effort to sweep the past away, more than 6000 houses were demolished. Whole communities disappeared, including Derwent Street, where Jo had been born. There was public outcry at this. The town's two-decade clearance plan included the replacement of Larkhill with the tower blocks still in evidence today and brought a cry for a stay of execution from townspeople, who didn't want their terraced-house communities destroyed. The council was caught between a rock and a hard place, for nearly a quarter of what was left could still be cat-egorised as slums and was earmarked for demolition. To achieve what they set out to do they realised they would have to out-build even the rate of build of the nation's new towns. Renovation grants provided the stop-gap. The programme was halted for a while and the overall strategy modified to include grants for renovation of existing dwellings.

Simultaneously, in a wholesale clearance and rebuild of the town centre, following plans un-veiled in 1955, the very same year that Jo's mother took half the family out of Blackburn, the River Blakewater around which the original settlement of Blackburn had been built was consigned to deepest memory, the idea being to build over it and make a new market and shopping centre that would return the town to its sixteenth-century reputation as the market town for East Lancashire.

The new centre was completed in three phases in the 1960s and 1970s. The last Easter Fair took place in April 1964, and on 30 December the same year, the old market clock-tower was felled. There couldn't have been a more symbolic moment.

In the same period there was an equally visible but very different sort of change going on in the town, a wholesale demographic change, the settlement of a whole new population – families from India, Pakistan, Bangladesh and Africa began pouring in.

When Jo left in 1955 there were only a few hundred Asians living in Blackburn. By 1970 there were well over 5000. Twenty years later there were nearly 20,000 resident in what had become the township of Blackburn with Darwen, and today the figure is 28,384, or 20.6% of the population.

In *Her Father's Sins*, Queenie overhears locals marvelling at the infusion:

> *'These past few years, since the start o' the break-up of the British Empire, the dark-skinned folk 'ave started trekking into our little island . . . an' it won't be long afore they come a flooding in, I'll tell yer!' Back came the reply, 'Aye! Well . . . they've every right, tha' knows!'*

*And when a third intervention related, 'If some-
body 'ad offered me the bloody Crown Jewels
some five years back, against a body swappin'
the land o' sunshine to come to Blackburn ...
I'd never 'a tekken the bet! Now would you
ever 'a thought it? Or you eh?' he asked, nodding his head to one and all, 'an' I'll tell you
some'at else! They reckon as there's nigh on
fifty dark-skinned families settled i' Blackburn
alone! My youngest came to close quarters wi'
a black face in Market Hall for the first time a'
Friday ... an' the missus says 'e set up such a
bawling it wer 'ard to tell who took fright most,
the young 'un or the poor unsuspecting fella!'
Then, supping his pint he shook his head, and
added, 'It's summat us shall all 'ave to get
used to, an' that's a fact!' A profound remark,
greeted with nods of resignation and a call
for another round of pints; after which, that
particular subject done with, the conversation
turned to the winning prowess of Blackburn
Rovers football team.*

There are other ethnic groups in Blackburn today
– Black African, Black Caribbean and Chinese, for
example – but their number is tiny by comparison
with Asians. Only the influx of the Irish, following
the terrible potato famine in Ireland a century earlier,
comes anywhere near it.

The potato harvest in Ireland had failed in 1845, 1846 and again in 1848. People had been left with nothing to eat and no way to make money to support themselves. Many wandered the countryside begging for food or work. Many starved to death. Those who could left Ireland in search of a better life. Blackburn, with its then buoyant cotton industry, had been a popular destination. In 1851 there were 2,505 Irish-born inhabitants of Blackburn, roughly three per cent of the population. In the following ten years this nearly doubled, and, since Irish families were traditionally large, the numbers that were born locally to these swelled the Irish population further, so that the true percentage of Irish in Blackburn by 1861 was well over ten per cent.

Economic and social factors likewise brought Asians to Blackburn from India and Pakistan, even as the town's traditional cotton industry waned, while political issues brought asylum-seekers from parts of Africa, particularly from Uganda. Inevitably, like the Irish before them, they took up the lower-paid jobs when they arrived, but it was the Asians who made the most indelible mark on the place, for theirs proved to be the stronger culture. Most of the Irish were Catholics, while most of the Asians were Muslim, but religion dominated every facet of the Asians' approach to life, whether they were Muslim, Hindu or Sikh, and as fast as the Blackburn skyline shed its chimneys, mosques became a part of it. Also,

Leaving home: Jo's mother was pregnant when she made the decision finally to leave her husband and Blackburn. 'She gathered us all together on the bus station, where they used to park the buses over night. She just drew us all together when dad had gone to work. I cried for weeks. I was fourteen, not a good time.'

In the 1960s, Jo's homeland underwent a transformation, but some street communities survived and from Dunstable in Bedfordshire, Jo 'longed to walk again the streets and ginnels of her beloved Blackburn,' as she wrote in *Let Loose the Tigers*.

'The worst thing they did to Blackburn was to take the market,' said Jo. 'They took the whole market area away, the clock and everything.'

One day, Jo's mother upped and left, and took her children to an estate 200 miles to the south, in Ridgmont, Buckinghamshire. Nothing could have been more different from her street life in Blackburn: 'My! This is a lovely place,' she remarked, looking from one side of the street to the other. The old square church with its pretty tower stood to the left of her, and to the right was an ancient inn with black-timbered gables and flower-filled gardens.' *Cradle of Thorns*

One of Jo's most recent novels, *The Beachcomber*, is set in West Bay, Dorset, a place of peace and regeneration for Jo since she spent childhood holidays there after the split from her father.

There was always a need to escape, even as a child. Blackpool lies on the coast west of Blackburn. When Jo first went with on a Ragged School outing as a child, 'God knows how long I stood there just staring at the space... I stood on the sand for ages and ages just looking, because you know at home the streets were very dark, the buildings, the cobbles.' She recalled the outing in *Her Father's Sins*, where, 'The tower of Blackpool rose up from the skyline like a giant twinkling ornament.'

Blackpool beach, a beauty uncovered. 'This vast space of water meeting with the sky. It was just... just mind boggling.'

To the south of Blackpool lies the flat expanse of Lytham St Anne's, where Maisie and her daughter, Sheila, are charged with keeping an immoral house in *Let Loose the Tigers*, and where Mary Honeywell retreats in *Bad Boy Jack* after deserting Robert Sullivan and throwing his life into disarray.

Just north of Blackburn lies the magnificent Forest of Bowland, where, in *Live the Dream*, Luke Hammond has a cabin 'nestling in the shadows of the fells'. Jo insists, 'If I had gone there as a child I would never have returned home again.'

Josephine Cox. For the writer there is a serious inability to bury the past, whatever joys or demons it may hold, and such a desire to re-visit it that the past often seems more real than the present. 'I wrote stories about the people I grew up with,' she says. 'Once I started, the words just flowed off the pages.'

because the Asians came from a variety of places with distinct cultures, they tended to settle accordingly, in distinct communities, and suddenly pockets of Blackburn changed dramatically to reflect their diverse mores.

The new Asian population was generally serious and industrious and not weighed down by the British tradition of worker exploitation, so that they made a more immediate play for a stake in the place than the Irish had by saving their money and buying property. By 1977, more than ninety per cent of the ethnic minority population of Blackburn owned their own houses. Any success they had may seem incredible, given that this new population was operating in a declining industry.

While all this was going on, Jo's visits to Blackburn had continued. She was amazed by what she saw and appalled by the town clearance programme. 'When I was growing up there, the centre had these lovely old buildings. Then, in the 1960s, they razed it to the ground and built these square, horrible blocks! The rebuilding was all going on when I was away, and I was shocked when I went back, and Derwent Street had gone, a complete area, a whole minefield of streets! They had all the flats there off Montague Street, and the first thing I thought was, where's the bike shop, the little old man who used to hire bikes out of there at fourpence a day? Where had he gone?

As a kid I would work all weekend collecting newspapers to take to the factory to get my fourpence and then I would go to the shop and hire my bike, proudly take it home to cycle to Accrington to see my granddad. I remember once I came out and my sister had pinched my bike and gone off on it and brought it back two minutes before it had to be returned. The worst thing they did to Blackburn was to take the market. They took the whole market area away, the clock and everything.'

For the writer there is a serious inability to bury the past, and such a desire to revisit it that it often seems more real than the present. Jo only truly returned to Blackburn when she visited it imaginatively in *Her Father's Sins*, and I put it to her that of all the novels that involve the heroine making a return to Blackburn, *Somewhere, Someday* seems the most true in terms of the author's emotional response.

In the novel, Kelly Wilson suffers a similar loss to Jo, though an even more dramatic one. Her father, the source of strife, has been murdered in the family house (No. 12 Johnson Street in the novel, which is Addison Street in reality). Her mother goes to prison for the murder, and Kelly leaves Blackburn.

I spent time at the top of Addison Street, staying in an Asian guest house nearby during my research. The street meets Preston New Road on the north boundary of the mill-colony into which Jo was born.

It is one of those high-up places from which Jo's heroines look out over Blackburn and drink deep of the spirit of the place.

'This street you are talking about in *Somewhere, Someday*,' Jo said. 'I used to play in that street when I was a child, and it is on a real steep brew, isn't it? Stand at the top and you can see right across the whole of Blackburn. I called it Johnson Street in the novel, but it is Addison Street in real life. The family of the children I played with used to live in the house at the very top. Ken and I were on a tour up north about seven years ago and as we drove past the top of the street I saw this house all boarded up. And I thought where have they gone? And if they've moved on, why is that house not being lived in? And it played on my mind because it was part of my life. So that is where the story came from. I thought, I am going to have someone going back to that house.'

Kelly returns to Blackburn, the site of her childhood trauma. 'I poured my own emotions into her going back,' Jo admits. 'You know, when I came back to see my father for the first time after he and my mam separated, there really was a milkman coming round the corner . . .'

She watched the milkman as he swung into the street, then reined in his horse to serve the many customers who stood, jug in hand, each awaiting her turn. He chatted awhile, and laughingly

*chucked the bairns under the chin, before meas-
uring out the milk from his churn with a ladle
. . . In her memory's eye, Kelly could see herself
in that queue. A small girl carrying a jug almost
as big as herself, she would dare to touch the
horse's chest and pat his face when he looked
down. If he kissed her for an apple, she would
screech with delight. Such vivid, precious times.*

Like Jo, when Kelly returns there are ghosts to lay,
'and the feelings were the same, they were transported into that street, what Kelly felt was what
I felt':

*When the moment came, and she was standing
at the top of Johnson Street, Kelly was filled
with a strange kind of calm, as though it wasn't
her standing there, but someone else. Someone
she didn't even know.*

*Mesmerised, she gazed at each house in turn;
all but one.*

*Deliberately she turned her back to it – the
house where she and her brother had lived with
their parents; the house she had loved, the
house she had feared. If she were to stretch out
her arm now, she could touch it, and she would.
She must! But, fearing her own emotions, she
prolonged the inevitable.*

Like an old friend, or enemy, it called to her,

daring her to turn and see. She so wanted to look at the house, at the small, significant things. She hoped the words her brother had scratched into the windowsill had lasted the test of time. Michael and Kelly for ever – he had written it with their mother's kitchen knife. No one had noticed; no one knew except she and her brother. Was it still there? Dare she look?

She remembered the door too, solid and permanent, as if it might be left standing long after the house and everyone in it had fallen away. She needed to see if the door was the same one that her father had put on after the old one warped with the weather; the door with the big, dark keyhole and a letter-box that sang in the wind. The door through which she and her loved ones had passed time and again.

It was stark in her mind now, that wonderfully familiar door made of dark, solid wood, with four panels and a small brass knocker in the shape of a crown. Oh yes, she longed to look on it, but try as she might, she did not quite dare.

Instead she roved her eyes over other familiar things: grubby, stone-framed windows; paving flags in long straight lines like little soldiers, some more worn than others; lampposts with stiff, inviting arms; and a road *filled with plump misshapen cobblestones that resembled new-baked loaves. Little had changed.*

Choking back a well of emotion, Kelly devoured it all. She had forgotten how it felt. Until now, she had not realised how much it meant to her.

After a moment, she raised her gaze and looked beyond the street to the distant view. As she did so, her heart turned somersaults.

Kelly had always thought this to be the most wonderful view in the world. Even though she had been a long time away, it had stayed in her mind's eye, etched on her soul for ever.

Now, in this unforgettable moment, she drank it in, her soul crying out with excitement. Almost as though she was being lifted from the ground, she felt herself fly, soaring with the view, down and away, over the heart of Blackburn town and beyond, to the hills. She saw the church spires and the towering cotton-mills, the endless, shifting sky spreading its fluttering wings over all below, and her quiet eyes knew it all.

This was what she remembered . . . grimy, smoky Blackburn town; so beautiful, it took her breath away.

'How I've missed you,' she sighed, and her heart was broken.

CHAPTER EIGHT

New Landscapes

Jo wrote *Somewhere, Someday* seven years ago, evincing the loss she felt so deeply following her alienation from her father and brothers and the land of her birth. But by the time she came to write it, she had already found another place to belong. Woburn Sands is one of the leafy villages close to Ridgmont, to which she first came with her mother half a century ago. One of her sons lives there also, the other in the next village. 'It is a hive of activity,' she has written, 'with a pretty old pub, ancient church, excellent school, parish council and a very close community . . . I have a real sense of belonging here. Ken and I moved away a few years ago, but it was only twenty-two months before we moved back again. Our former house, which Ken had virtually rebuilt, came back on the market. Ken said, "Let's go and see if the magic is still there." We came back and the house welcomed us. A month later we moved in.'

It is all a far cry from the landscape of her birth,

but she meets it with similar excitement: 'Even today I get a rush of joy from seeing animals in the fields. There is a field opposite my house and every spring I see newborn lambs and horses. From my back window I can see the whole of Aylesbury Vale.' Husband Ken had a summerhouse built in their orchard, which has views over the entire vale.

These feelings go into her novels just as her feelings for the Blackburn of old do. Barney Davidson is Leonard Maitland's farm manager at Far Crest Farm in nearby Salford in Jo's latest novel, *The Journey*. Leonard's wife prefers to live in the town, but it is Jo, their creator, who settles the argument: 'You can have no idea of what it feels like to see the harvest being brought in, or to stride the fields on a winter's morning, when the snow lies deep in the ditches and the trees bend and dip with the weight . . .'

Recently, the broadcaster Sue Lawley detected a drift away from Blackburn as inspiration. In response, Jo accepted that she has set *The Journey* and other books in the area where she now lives, but claimed, 'There's the same strength in the characters, there's the same heartbreak, and it doesn't matter the setting. Sometimes I'll stray a little and write of other things, but always I come back to my roots . . . And that's when I'm happiest.'

There is perhaps a widening of focus, a sense that landscape, be it urban or rural, is not her first call as a writer, a mature feeling that the slum terraces of Blackburn are not the sole provenance of pain, suffering, love, discord and resolution, though Blackburn formed this unique, self-contained and accessible environment in which she could deal with the emotional contours that define her own inner landscape.

In December 2002, Jo's husband, Ken, the man she loved and with whom she had grown up and made a family, the man she once described to me as 'my best friend and right arm', and who I knew as a kind, considerate and thoughtful man, unexpectedly died of cancer. It was a brutal shock. 'Since losing Ken,' she said to me recently, 'life takes on a different colour.'

Thousands of readers wrote letters that moved her to tears. Through her regular newsletter, *Chatterbox*, she shared her feelings about how hard it is going on without him. Inevitably, Ken's passing would affect her writing.

In *Live the Dream* (published in 2004 and written a year earlier), Jo gives us sensitive, caring Luke Hammond, who has a brush-making factory in Blackburn, and young, carefree Amy and her friend Daisy – characters who 'match like a pair of socks, one blue, one red', as Jo put it to me. Luke, Amy and Daisy and the Blackburn men the two girls meet, Jack and Roy, seem to provide secure anchorage for Jo in the culture that formed her.

Publication followed that of *The Beachcomber* in 2003, which is set not in Blackburn but in a place that also brought back happy memories for Jo, memories of idyllic caravan holidays that she and Ken shared with their sons when they were young. The novel is set in West Bay, Dorset, a stunning section of the Jurassic coast between Bridport and Lyme Regis.

'West Bay has changed,' said Jo when I asked her about it. 'When the children were small we had a caravan down there. You could sit on a little jetty area and watch the fishermen on the pier, and we loved that. As you go into West Bay there's a big house on the right, and it was very run down. I've used that. I have resurrected that house. It is Tom Arnold's house in the novel, a house of love. When the book came out, someone wrote to me to say that they have taken away the high walls that create the narrow tunnel of water over which Tom goes out on his boat. The water used to rush through there, frightening. Now, apparently, they have done away with those walls and opened it right out to make it a harbour. But there's still the caravan site, even the post box and the pub, and the place where Samantha was attacked is exactly as I described it.'

The novel's dedication reads: 'This book, and every book I will ever write, is for Ken, a man amongst men, my soul mate and inspiration forever.' How could it not be influenced by him?

The novel opens with a tragedy. Successful architect Tom Arnold is driving with his family when his car is run off the road by an unknown driver, who doesn't stop. Tom's family are killed. He survives. He draws from this senseless loss the knowledge that, 'We're never "in control" ... He knew all about that. He knew from experience how one minute everything was perfect, filled with love and joy, and, before you knew it, your whole world was turned upside down.'

Tom Arnold, like Jo, his creator, had looked to everyone as if he'd 'got the world at his feet', and he had loved his family 'with a passion that frightened him'. Now, there can be 'no respite from the shocking memories. Day or night, asleep or awake, they were etched on his soul.' He lashes out, swears he will find the murderous bastard who killed his family, and then recognises, 'I need ... to control the hatred. Right now, the hatred is controlling me.'

It takes Kathy Wilson from Acton in London to help Tom settle these issues of bereavement. Kathy is immediately identified with Jo because she has lost her father. Like Jo's own family, Kathy's has been split asunder: her sister, Samantha, and her mother, Irene, on one side; Kathy and her dad on the other. However, Kathy's background couldn't be more different from Jo's. She was brought up in 'a pretty four-bedroomed place ... in a nice part of Kensington, situated in a tree-lined road where the houses sat well back amongst beautifully tended gardens . . .' Also, Kathy's father has died rather than being deserted. But none of this matters; the psychology of the two situations remains similar. Both daughters are bereft of the father, and in both cases there is serious difficulty in accepting the situation. 'For one heart-stopping minute as she glanced towards the house, Kathy could see her father standing on the doorstep, waving a welcome, his smile enveloping her like sunshine after rain.' It will take Tom to help Kathy forget her loss.

Kathy inherits Barden House in West Bay in her father's will. It is a place where he had been ecstatically happy with a woman called Liz, who is everything that his difficult wife, Irene, Kathy's mother, had not been. On arrival, Kathy meets seventy-three-year-old Jasper Hardcastle, a dead-ringer for Jo's Granddad Harrison and long-term resident of West Bay. He had 'been to West Bay as a lad with me mam and dad . . . had the time o' me life, I did, an' I never forgot. Well, I just kinda wandered back . . . got casual work . . .' Jasper tells Kathy that Barden House 'was filled with priceless things . . . with happiness and love. For your father and his sweetheart, every day was a new adventure.' It is the house of love that Jo remembers was hers with Ken all those years ago. Later, Kathy is told by an old man, 'He gave you this 'ouse 'cause he wanted you to find the same happiness he knew with Liz.'

270

Although initially shocked on hearing about her father's infidelity, Kathy doesn't blame her father 'for wanting to get away from Mother . . . I'm glad you found someone who treated you right . . . somebody who loved you the way you deserved to be loved.' She dedicates herself to recovering the beauty and happiness of the relationship in his memory. She is determined to 'restore this lovely house to its former beauty . . .' It is a kind of monument to him.

The Beachcomber is a tender novel at times, and Jo's faithful readers will realise that she is letting them in, at a very personal level, to the workings of her heart. But the emotions of her characters seem almost more important than the characters themselves, even independent of them. The sense of loss of the father figure is felt most painfully not by the daughter but, more touchingly, by the father's love-child, young Robbie, who is in fact named after the father, further to diminish the importance of individuals over the emotions they express:

> *A sadness touched his voice. 'Mummy says we might go back one day, but not yet.'*
>
> *The old man's heart was sore. 'I'm sure yer mammy means to take yer back . . .'*
>
> *The boy looked up, his eyes moist with tears but a smile on his face. 'Oh, Jasper, will she take me back? Will she?'*
>
> *'That's summat for your mammy to decide,*

son.' He had more sense than to raise the boy's hopes too high.

Suddenly his heart lurched when the boy asked in all innocence, 'Then, will Daddy come back?'

What is so crushingly sad about this is that the reader knows that Robbie's father is already dead, gone forever. He is never coming back. Robbie's loss is never to be assuaged.

'Never coming back' is what this novel is about. Loss is ubiquitous: Tom's loss, Kathy's loss, Robbie's loss, and of course Jo's own loss. Everywhere there is loss, and everyone who experiences loss is drawn to West Bay and to Jasper, the Granddad Harrison figure, who affirms the positive, unifying, healing qualities of the place.

There is, mercifully, hope in the very tendency of *The Beachcomber* to focus on the emotional dimension almost at the expense of individual character. For, loss itself conveys something of what has been lost; there is an inheritance. Something inherent in the relationships – Tom's with his family, Kathy's and Robbie's with their father, and his with Liz – survives and is symbolised by this house of love, which is Kathy's inheritance. It is as if knowledge of this creeps up on Jo as stealthily as it does on her heroine:

'It was your house, Dad,' she whispered, 'yours and hers. And now it's mine.' She caught her breath in wonder and blew it out in relief. 'I need a while to take it all in,' she thought.

The Beachcomber was followed by two other stories of love and courage, *Lovers and Liars* and *The Journey*. Again, loss conveys the nature of true love. In the first, the love between Emily Ramsden and John Hanley is so deep and pure that even their eventual spouses accept that it takes priority over their feelings for them. That Emily and John marry other partners is their fate, a destiny determined by the outrageous rape of Emily by her uncle, which leaves her pregnant with Cathleen, who John assumes wrongly is Emily's child by Danny Williams, the man who has been kind to her while John is away at sea earning enough money to wed and care for her. Jo's story turns on this tragic misconception, fed to John by his Aunt Lizzie, who is, in Jo's words, 'a dear misguided woman who thinks she's acting for the best' when she deliberately comes between the two people she cares for.

Again, paternity is a constant issue, not only the question of the identity of Cathleen's father – no one other than her mother Emily knows that she is the product of rape by Uncle Clem – but also the disappearance of Emily's own father, and even the loss of John's Liverpool landlady Harriet Witherington's father. A daughter's loss of her father is everywhere in the book, but now it is joined by a woman's loss of the man she loves – Emily's loss of John Hanley, and her mother's loss of her husband – and the need for Emily and her mother to be strong in the absence of their men. Again, Jo alludes to the real-life context in which she is writing this: 'This book was written during a time in my life when I needed friends and family like never before . . .'

When John Hanley returns from the sea, he observes Emily from a spinney on top of a hill. He gazes down upon her, her child and the man he now assumes is her child's father, from afar. The tragedy of John Hanley is that henceforth he must forever look down upon her from afar, in his mind's eye. He becomes as it were a spirit presence. He exists for Emily, but only in her heart.

As he got to the top of the hill, he could see the curl of smoke rising from the Ramsdens' chimney. 'I'm here, my darling,' he murmured, his heart bouncing inside him. 'I'm home.'

He could barely wait to throw his arms round her and hold her tight. Thinking about it, he quickened his steps. He was so close. So tantalisingly close.

It was when he got to the spinney that he heard the laughter. Curious, he slowed his step. Some instinct kept him back, partly hidden by the overhanging branches, yet able to see down to the farm.

And what he saw was like ice-cold spray, flung in his face by an angry sea.

Not knowing what to think or how to deal with it, he stayed there, out of sight; watching the scene unfold below him, and with every minute his dream slipping away.

At first his gaze fell on Emily, and his love for her was all-consuming. With the chill March daylight glinting in her golden-brown hair and that familiar, lovely face, she was everything he remembered. And yet she was different somehow, though for the moment he could not tell why.

Curious, he followed her proud gaze. He saw the child run towards her; he saw how she opened her arms and caught that tiny bundle to her heart, her eyes alight with love – and when in that moment she shared the laughter with the child, she seemed to John to be the most beautiful, fulfilled woman on God's earth.

Slowly, when the truth began to dawn, the revelation was crippling.

For a moment he could not think straight, though his every nerve-ending was telling him that this little girl was Emily's child. But how could that be? The conductor's words ran through his mind. 'How can you be sure she hasn't found another fella?'

Torn by what he was seeing, he could not move away.

From the corner of his eye he caught sight of the stranger as he walked towards Emily and the child. He saw him smile and open his arms to take her from Emily; she released the child without a moment's hesitation. The man swung the child round, while Emily laughed out loud at the little one's delight.

After a while, Emily approached the man and collected the child into her arms. As she did so, the child uplifted her face for a kiss from the man. Obligingly, he cupped her tiny face in his hands to gently kiss her on the forehead . . .

Unable to look any longer, John turned away, his heart breaking.

It is as if Hanley is seeing the scene played out in a parallel universe. He can see but he cannot reach out to the woman he loves. Life has moved on. He is looking at the future. He is no longer a participant in Emily's time. His fate is sealed when Aunt Lizzie confirms his worst fears that the child is Emily's and the stranger's.

In fact, as we know, this isn't the case, but life must go on, and eventually Emily does marry the stranger, Danny Williams, even though she doesn't love him like she loves John:

> *I still love you, John Hanley, she thought.*
> *Danny is a good man – a kind man. He wants*
> *to wed me and raise Cathleen as his own. He*
> *has a business, and money enough to help us*
> *be rid of Clem Jackson, and yet he asks for*
> *little in return. And still I can't bring myself to*
> *say yes, because all I can think of is you ...*
> *Emily began to cry; soft, wet tears trickling*
> *down her face and her heart aching with mem-*
> *ories of John and the way it used to be. Why*
> *did you leave me? Caught by the breeze, her*
> *words were soon gentled away.*

John goes away and teams up with his old ship-mate Archie in a plan to start up a wagon-making business on the Leeds–Liverpool canal. Archie used to drive wagons for Thwaites's Brewery in Blackburn – 'delivered all over the North, from when I was little more than a lad, right up to the day before I signed my name to be a sailor.' Together they make it a success and John eventually finds himself a wife, Rosie Taylor, who works for the family barge company. He teams up with her in business and in marriage, though, again, he does not love her like he loves Emily.

Eventually, however, it becomes clear that Danny,

Emily, John and Rosie are 'all caught up in a mess of Lizzie's own making . . . It could have been different, lass, if only I hadn't interfered . . . Y'see it were me as sent John away.'

Inevitably the two couples – Danny and Emily, John Hanley and Rosie – come together, and so powerful is the magnetism between Emily and John that Danny and Rosie can only step aside and let it flow. They 'saw it happen and they were afraid . . .' The lovers inhabit an interior world and are lost to the real world. It is not the real world, for we know that in the real world Emily will return to Danny and John to Rosie. But it is a world no less real to Emily and John – quite distinct, to them more real than real, a place where terrible love-loss is made good.

This night, this love, and the knowledge that the love would always be there, drawing them together, yet keeping them apart. It was how it should be.

Jo is working things out between the lines of this book, trying to come to terms with personal tragedy.

She would never forget her first love. They had been two young people setting out on life's journey. Two lovers who had shared a dream and lost it, but in the losing had found some-

thing else. The love that had grown between them was still there, but it was a different love now. It was a strong, binding love that would go on for as long as they lived.

The love of friendship.

A precious thing, after all.

In 2005, Jo's novel *The Journey* again explored the theme of the death of a loved one, but this has special significance, for it came to Jo unbidden. 'Sometimes,' she tells us, 'something happens that you can't explain, yet it is so powerful you cannot ignore it. It can be magical and wonderful, and at the same time a little disturbing ... About a year ago, I started working on a story about a darling woman who is deeply unsettled by something she finds out. Her past is not what it seemed, she is not what she imagined, and so she sets out to set the record straight. I was already deeply engrossed in writing the second chapter [when] one night, after working late, I awoke in the early hours (as I often do) with another story filling my mind. Half asleep, I scribbled for a while and went back to sleep.

'When I awoke in the morning, I was astonished to find that I had filled four A4 pages with the outline of a complete story from beginning to end. I had assumed what I had written was about the book I was working on, because you do it half asleep, but when I read what I had written I was amazed because it was the total skeleton of a brand new book. I have no idea where it came from. It must have been ticking away in the back of my head somewhere. There was the period in which it was set, the actual geographical setting, the characters, and something else which I could not put my finger on. There was a kind of urgency about it. I'm always excited when I start another story, but this time it was more than that. Try as I might, I could not put it out of my mind. Usually when I wake and make notes about ideas for other stories, I can put the notes on file and go back to them when I've finished the book I'm working on. This time, the story and the characters would not let me be, so, in spite of a tight deadline, I put away the story I was working on and began *The Journey*.

'I wrote it like someone driven and when I finished it I was mentally and emotionally exhausted, and utterly overawed by the power of the story. In fact, when I came to what I thought was the end, neither the story nor the characters would leave me. So, I am now engrossed in what I imagine will be the conclusion, *Journey's End*.

'I have so many questions – why did the story present itself to me in its entirety? Why have I been more excited about this book than any other? Why could I not put it aside? Most of all, why has this story evoked in me deep feelings of humility and joy?'

The period in which *The Journey* is set is the 1950s; the novel opens in 1952 and flashes back to the 1930s. The setting is Salford, Bedfordshire, a little village close to the Ampthill and Ridgmont of *Cradle of Thorns*, and near where Jo lives today, the scene of some of the happiest days of Jo's marriage to Ken.

We are first introduced to the characters in a graveyard. Ben Morris sees two women paying their respects at the grave of one Barney Davidson, on which is written: '1890–1933 A Man of Courage He Made the Greatest Sacrifice of All'.

Ben lives and works at nearby Far Crest Farm, and, like Tom Arnold, the hero of *The Beachcomber*, he had earlier been a respected architect. Also like Tom, Ben has been forced into embarking on a new stage of his life, which has been blighted by tragedy, not a death this time but the infidelity of his wife. One day Ben came home to find his wife in bed with his ex-business partner, Peter.

Inexplicably drawn to the two women in the graveyard, Ben follows them to Knudsden House, their home. In time, he discovers that the younger of the two women, Mary, is the other woman, Lucy's, daughter by the late Barney Davidson, whose grave they have just visited.

This is merely the preamble to Jo's story, which concerns what led to the inscription on the tombstone – what inspired Barney's courage and sacrifice.

The secret is revealed in flashback, and the novel ends as it begins.

Driven by Jo's admission that she only ever writes about things that have 'happened to me or my family or to my friends' and the knowledge that, as in the case of *Scarlet*, she is writing from her deep unconscious, we can expect a highly personal novel. Immediately, there are indicators that this is so.

She dedicates the novel to Ken. The name of the hero of the piece is Barney, the name of her own father. In the story, Ben reminds Mary of her father, Barney, and she takes to him. The depth of Lucy's love for Barney is seen to be akin to Mary's love for Ben. Family friend Adam Chives detects 'the start of another deep and special love' and that 'Ben truly belonged here'. We have already noted the identification of father and husband in *The Beachcomber*. Here, it is explicit.

> *Barney Davidson was a very special man. Not because he was handsome or rich, or even because he was exceptional in ways we mere mortals might understand . . . No! He was more than that. He was deep and kind . . . Sometimes, words alone can never describe someone.*

This was Jo's Ken all over. Again, Barney, like Ken, has two sons, Ronnie and Thomas, and, like Ken, he is a family man. He 'loved family mealtimes, when everyone sat down together and talked, when laughter and noise and arguments happened, and you felt as though you belonged to something very special.'

There is terrible grief at the loss of Barney: 'All the men in the world rolled into one could never replace her beloved Barney . . . Half-asleep, her brain numbed by the sedative, she called out his name. "Barney!" Her voice and her heart broke, and she could speak no more.' She takes a photo of him and holds it to the bedside lamp: 'Lucy could hardly see it for the tears that stung from her eyes and ran unheeded down her face. "Oh Barney, dear Barney!" The sobbing was velvet-soft. No one heard. No one knew. No one *ever* knew. For nearly twenty years, she had kept his face alive in her.'

In the context, this scene is almost too touching to bear, but what the story releases in Jo is not only grief but 'deep feelings of humility and joy'. What Jo's novel tells us, what it tells all her readers who have lost loved ones, is that death releases truths which can get lost in the sheer *business* of life.

The extraordinary thing is that we learn of Barney's qualities, in particular his capacity for love, not in the arms of Lucy, who first introduces us to them and we assume is his wife, but in the arms of Lucy's friend, Vicky, who was in fact Barney's wife before he and Lucy met. In flashback, we learn that the love between Barney and Vicky was 'a deep, everlasting love, and one which Lucy sensed neither she nor countless others would ever experience in their whole lives.' Later, Lucy talks to Vicky about this and Vicky confesses: 'Sometimes it frightens me, the way Barney believes we'll always be together. The thing is, Lucy, when you're part of each other, like me and Barney, there can never be a happy ending. Someone is bound to be sad at the end of it all . . . You see, when either of us is taken, the one left behind will be totally lost.'

Then Lucy is given sanctuary in Barney and Vicky's home at Overhill Farm and herself falls in love with Barney, ending up with him when Vicky goes to America. How this came about, and how Jo manages to preserve Barney's heroic qualities and the reader's identification with and approval of Lucy in the light of the fact that she runs off with her best friend's husband, is testimony to Jo's skills as a writer. It is not, in fact, the only time a sympathetic character is allowed to desecrate a love that is hallowed in one of her novels. Most recently it occurred in *The Woman Who Left*, where the idyllic love match is between Ben and Louise, and Louise flouts it in an elicit affair with Eric Forester, gamekeeper of Samlesbury Manor, the man who benefits from Ben's loss of the family home. Later, Ben commits suicide. In *The Journey*, the betrayal occurs in less reprehensible circumstances, and for a purpose. The wife, Vicky, has already left for America and is at least out of reach, and Barney, as we now discover, has little time to live.

Barney is a tenant farmer at Overhill and events conspire to effect the Davidsons' removal from the farm to another property belonging to Leonard Maitland, Overhill's owner and close friend of the Davidsons, in America. It is then that Barney learns that he has a life-threatening disease, a heart disease as it happens. The prognosis is not good. There is little that can be done . . .

In a kind of half-drunken stupor Barney left the surgery and made his way to the horse and cart, which he had tethered outside. Without his usual greeting to the old horse, he climbed aboard, took up the reins and clicking the horse away, sat back on his slatted wooden bench and turned his thoughts to Vicky and the family.

As he left the village behind and came into the open countryside, he stopped the horse in its tracks, and climbing down off the bench, stood at the top of the valley, from where he could see the whole world.

He stood for a long time, his mind numbed and his heart sore, and when the doctor's words flooded back . . . 'It's possible you may enjoy a few good years': . . . he lifted his face to the skies and with tears streaming down his face, he accused the Great Master somewhere in the heavens: 'Every step of my life I've always trusted You, and now when my life seems to be taking a turn for the better, You snatch it away.' Anger roared through him. 'WHAT TERRIBLE THING DID I DO TO DESERVE THIS?' Sobbing, he fell to the ground.

In his mind's eye he could see Vicky, and his children. He saw the joy in their eyes and the excitement in their voices as they spoke of their imminent new life in Boston, and it was as though a knife was twisting his soul.

Barney chooses to suffer silently. Under sentence of death, he thinks first not for himself. It is his family he fears for . . . 'I don't know how to prepare them . . . We've allus been close – too close, mebbe, because that makes it all the more painful.'

It is in the manner in which Barney decides to handle this that brings his courage and sacrifice to the fore. Like Robbie's father in *The Beachcomber*, Barney would rather die out of sight than let his much-loved family suffer his slow decline. Jo tries to explain to me: 'He could not lean on his wife because he could not share his suffering with her.'

Barney, terminally ill but with some time yet to live, de-camps from Overhill Farm and deliberately – really heartlessly, and on the basis that you have to be cruel to be kind – sets his wife against him. Vicky, Ronnie and Thomas leave without him for America and a new life. Barney does this with a clear conscience. He knows that Leonard Maitland cares deeply for Vicky and, although he also doubts that Vicky would return his feelings, by clearing himself out of the way he feels he is paving the way for Leonard to look after his wife.

I began to see what Jo was getting at. Barney had sacrificed his own ego for the happiness of the woman he loved. Sacrifice indeed: it did not matter that his wife thought badly of him. He wanted her to, he needed her to. He had transferred the loss she would have felt to himself. 'I wanted the cover for *The Journey* to show the solitude and loneliness of Barney as the ship took his family away from him forever,' explained Jo. 'It is such a lonely picture.' Later, Barney puts himself in Lucy's care and eventually Lucy has the baby she wants by him – Mary – whom we met at the start of the novel.

But why Jo's 'deep feelings of humility and joy' at what Barney did? Some sort of response from the author was to be expected, given that the story arrived unbidden, but humility and joy . . . ? It was as if her 'dream' had revealed something of importance to her, something personally relevant.

'You are right,' I said to her. 'It takes enormous courage not to share one's own suffering and not to lean on the one you love.'

She said: 'Barney was a very special man. There's a lot of my Ken in that man . . .'

I left it there.

What we see in *The Journey* is an imaginative transition that has been brewing through Jo's most recent novels and comes to fruition there. As a writer, she is now dealing not with the landscape of Blackburn, nor with the landscape of Bedfordshire or Dorset. She is dealing with her own inner landscape, both conscious and unconscious. In a sense she always has been, but realising this is the point of her own creative journey so far, and now, understanding the process, and in spite of the title of her newest novel – *Journey's End* – the future promises much more.

NOVELS BY JOSEPHINE COX

1987   Her Father's Sins
1988   Let Loose the Tigers
1989   Angels Cry Sometimes
1989   Take This Woman
1990   Whistledown Woman
1991   Outcast
1991   Alley Urchin
1992   Vagabonds
1992   Don't Cry Alone
1993   Jessica's Girl
1993   Nobody's Darling
1994   Born to Serve
1994   More than Riches
1995   A Little Badness
1995   Living a Lie
1996   The Devil You Know
1996   A Time for Us
1997   Cradle of Thorns
1997   Miss You Forever
1998   Love Me or Leave Me
1998   Tomorrow the World

1999   The Gilded Cage
1999   Somewhere, Someday
2000   Rainbow Days
2000   Looking Back
2001   Let it Shine
2001   The Woman Who Left
2002   Bad Boy Jack
2003   The Beachcomber
2004   Lovers and Liars
2004   Live the Dream
2005   The Journey
2006   Journey's End

As Jane Brindle
1991   Scarlet
1992   No Mercy
1994   The Tallow Image
1995   No Heaven, No Hell
1997   The Seeker
1998   The Hiding Game

ACKNOWLEDGEMENTS

I would like to thank Josephine Cox's publishers, HarperCollins and Headline, for making this book possible, and Diana Rushton and Alan Duckworth at the Local Studies Department of the Blackburn Library, who guided my research and supplied many of the black and white photographs. Besides Charles Tiplady's recently recovered, nineteenth-century diary of the town, Alan Duckworth's *Aspects of Blackburn* was essential research. Similar help and source material came from Nick Harling at the Blackburn Museum & Art Gallery and from Albert Branscombe of the Local History Society.

I have already acknowledged Derek Beattie's *Blackburn: The Development of a Lancashire Cotton Town* (Ryburn Publishing, 1992) as the most authoritative modern history, and repeat my indebtedness to his research and acumen. *Poets and Poetry of Blackburn, 1793–1902* by George Hull (J & G Toulmin, 1902) was another eye-opener; working-class Blackburn poets draw together so many of the themes of the present book. Other crucial sources were *The Road To Nab End* by William Woodruff (Eland, 1993), *Working Children in Nineteenth-Century Lancashire*, edited by Michael Winstanley (Lancashire County Books, 1995), *20th-Century Blackburn* by Andrew Taylor (Wharncliffe Books, 2000), and *Images of East Lancashire* by Eric Leaver (copyright *Lancashire Evening Telegraph*, published by Breedon Books, 1993).

Amongst the black and whites the stunning street scenes of the 1960s by Shirley Baker deserve special mention. Readers may know her books, *Street Photographs. Manchester & Salford* (Bloodaxe, 1989) and *Streets & Spaces* (Lowry Press, 2000). Other photographic sources to whom I am indebted include the British Waterways Board; the Documentary Photographic Archive of the Greater Manchester County Record Office; the Guardian Media Group plc; Lancashire County Library; Burnley Library; The Lancashire Evening Telegraph; the Manchester Local Studies Unit, Central Library, Manchester; the North West Film Archive, Manchester; and Oldham Metropolitan Borough Leisure Services, Local Studies Library. The photograph of West Bay, Dorset is by Ian Britton (www.freeform.co.uk).

Above all, I would like to thank Josephine Cox, whose contribution lies at the very heart of the book.

INDEX

293

☐ **The Journey** Josephine Cox 0-00-714616-7		£6.99
☐ **Live the Dream** Josephine Cox 0-00-714613-2		£6.99
☐ **Lovers and Liars** Josephine Cox 0-00-714610-8		£6.99
☐ **The Beachcomber** Josephine Cox 0-00-714607-8		£6.99

Total cost _____

10% discount _____

Final total _____

To purchase by Visa/Mastercard/Switch simply call
08707871724 or fax on **08707871725**